*An Anthology of
Finnish Folktales*

An Anthology of
Finnish Folktales

Edited and translated by
Helena Henderson

Introduction by
Dr Pirkko-Liisa Rausmaa

welsh academic press

Cardiff

Published in Wales by Welsh Academic Press, an imprint of

Ashley Drake Publishing Ltd
PO Box 733
Cardiff
CF14 7ZY

www.welsh-academic-press.wales

First published as *The Maiden Who Rose From the Sea and other Finnish Folktales* (Hisarlik Press, 1992: 1 874312 01 X).

Published as An Anthology of Finnish Folktales
(Welsh Academic Press, 2013: 978-1-86057-083-4).
Second edition, with the original 1992 layout and artwork, published 2025.
Paperback: 978-1-86057-177-0
eBook: 978-1-86057-176-3

British Library Cataloguing-in-Publication Data.
A CIP catalogue for this book is available from the British Library.

Typeset by Prepress Plus Technologies, www.prepressplustechnologies.com
Cover design by the Books Council of Wales, Aberystwyth

To Sacha

Contents

Jokes and Anecdotes

Introduction

The Folklore Archive of the Finnish Literature Society (*Suomalaisen Kirjallisuuden Seura*, or SKS) in Helsinki, which is the central archive of the Finnish folk tradition collections, houses an unusually large number of folktales compared to similar collections in other countries. This is not because traditions of storytelling or knowledge of folktales were more widespread in Finland than elsewhere in the world; if anything, it is because of the geographical isolation of the country. Storytelling as a living tradition was preserved longer in Finland than in many other countries which more readily came into contact with a civilization that destroyed oral tradition. On the other hand, Finnish scholars were quick to react to international trends.

As early as the beginning of the nineteenth century a systematic and concentrated effort to preserve the folk tradition began, inspired by Central European Romanticism. The main impetus came from the founding of the Finnish Literature Society in 1831, and from the activities within the society of Elias Lönnrot, the compiler of the Finnish national epic *Kalevala*. At the beginning of the nineteenth century, as a result of wars, Finland was separated from Sweden and annexed to the Russian Empire as a Grand Duchy. Russification of the country and its integration with Russia posed a real danger, and the need for culture and literature in the Finnish language became obvious. There was a growing awareness of Finland's uniqueness, and a growing spirit of national awakening. Thus the recognition of a country's own oral tradition and its value and, especially, the acquisition of its own national epic were of crucial importance for the birth of the Finnish identity, and later, indirectly, even for the independence of Finland.

Folktales as well as ancient epic and lyric poetry were collected and recorded from the very beginning. We are fortunate that the work of recording folktales had begun while they were still known and were being told all over Finland. In 1852 the first collection of Finnish folktales, *Suomen kansan satuja ja tarinoita*, edited by Eero Salmelainen, was published; these tales reflect the folksy narrative style and tradition far more faithfully than most contemporary folktale publications in other countries.

Folklore collecting, which continues to this day, has seen contributions from a large and enthusiastic body of ordinary men and women alongside professional researchers and students. The collections of the SKS Folklore Archive have grown so large that it is now believed to be the largest folklore archive in the world. At present its collections are estimated at around three million manuscript notes in total; in addition to this, there are ca 15,000 sound and video recordings and around 80,000 photographs. There are around 90,000 manuscript notes of folktales and anecdotes. All of the tales in the present anthology come from the manuscript collection of the Folklore Archive.

FINNISH FOLKTALE SCHOLARSHIP

The large collections of folk material in Finland greatly influenced early international folklore research. The so-called historical-geographical method dominant in international folktale scholarship in the early part of this century is often referred to as the

Finnish method. Julius Krohn and, especially, his son Kaarle Krohn (who himself assembled large collections of folk traditions on his field-trips) developed a research method which sought to determine the origin and migratory route of individual items of tradition. As the method required as extensive and complete a body of variants as possible, it encouraged and accelerated the work of preserving folklore in Finland and elsewhere.

Kaarle Krohn used the historical-geographical method in his doctoral thesis dealing with animal tales, *Bär (Wolf) und Fuchs* (*Bear [Wolf] and Fox*, 1889), and his colleague Antti Aarne subsequently made the method better known in a series of monographs. In order to facilitate easier identification of tales in the collections, Antti Aarne devised a system of tale-types in 1910. This classification, which was also intended for international use, was based on the Finnish folktale collections supplemented by the collections of the Danish folklorist S. Grundtvig and the folktale publications of the Brothers Grimm. Each story deemed to have an independent existence in tradition was assigned a number. The tales are divided into the three broad categories of Animal Tales (Types 1–299), Ordinary Folktales (Types 300–1199) and Jokes and Anecdotes (Types 1200–2499); these categories are further subdivided into groups like Magic Tales (300–749), Tales of the Stupid Ogre (1000-1199), Numskull Stories (1200-1349), etc. The system, which continues to be very useful, particularly with regard to European material, was later expanded and supplemented by the American folklorist Stith Thompson in *The Types of the Folk-Tale* (1956).

Finnish folktales are closely connected with the

European folktale tradition. The greatest number of Finnish tales have been adopted from the West through Sweden; a small number in Northern Finland came through Norway. The tales have often been preserved in the Finnish tradition in forms much closer to early versions than the more developed versions elsewhere in Scandinavia. Many tales have been recorded in Finland which have all but disappeared elsewhere in Scandinavia. In some cases, however, tales have developed directions of their own and have thus acquired completely new features. This tendency has been further influenced by the absorption of traditions from the East. These Eastern folktales, primarily of Russian origin, depart in their type selection and their narrative style from that of their Western counterparts in many respects.

The narrative style of the Eastern Finnish tales is colourful, romantic and imaginative; the plot meanders unexpectedly and easily merges with other tales. Tales from Western Finland are shorter, sometimes slightly dry, but clear and factual and, possibly, more humorous than the Eastern ones. All in all, the body of Finnish folktales, which is composed of material derived from two directions, is exceptionally rich and versatile with regard to both the number of tale-types and the variety of narrative styles, and thus offers interesting material for the scholar and the general reader alike.

ANIMAL TALES

A striking feature of the Finnish material is the large number of animal tales. Nearly twice as many types of animal tale are found as in the other Scandinavian countries; about 130 different animal tale-types are known in Finland. The most popular and frequent animals in these tales are the fox, the bear, the wolf, and the rabbit. Domestic animals are represented by the horse, the cat and the dog. Alongside these homely and familiar creatures, we see lions venturing in the Finnish forests, an indication of the southerly origin of many of these animal tales that were adopted in the North.

The morality of the animal tales clearly differs from that of the other tales, where evil is always punished and good rewarded. In the animal tales, the honest and benevolent (if somewhat stupid) bear, for example, finds itself time after time the victim of the schemes of the cunning and treacherous fox. The strong representation of animal tales in the collections may also be explained by the fact that they were remembered for much longer than other tales, because they were also told to children; other tales were more the pastime of the adults.

ORDINARY FOLKTALES

The most typical feature in the body of folktales, however, are the so-called Tales of Magic, of which there are ca 140 different types known in Finland. For the most part the tales represent those also known elsewhere in Europe, but have in many instances evolved a direction of their own and gained strong local colour.

The inhabitants of the distant backwoods found it difficult to imagine, for instance, what a king's castle looked like and what life at court was like. Thus the royal dwelling might in the stories appear as a large farm-house where the king is seated at the top of the table just like any farm-owner would; the princess herself would bring a cup of coffee to the visiting shepherd, and the queen might be washing her son's shirts by the lake. The sauna is just as important a Finnish element in the tales as it still is to the Finns today. Many events take place in the sauna; in particular, this is where the offspring of both the queen and the country girl alike are born.

The creature of evil is generally called the devil, who nevertheless may appear as one of many different creatures: a troll, a giant, a dragon, a monster in the form of an animal, a human in possession of evil powers, or the devil of the Christian faith. In this compilation, tales like *The Bird Bride*, *The Witch and the Sister of Nine Brothers* or *The Maiden Who Rose From the Sea*, for example, represent tale-types containing primitive elements which are rare in Europe. All feature mythical and magical elements which point to ancient folk beliefs, and the latter two also contain rhymes in the old Finnish metre (the so-called Kalevala-metre) and rhythmic cliché expressions.

JOKES AND ANECDOTES

The number of humorous tales and anecdotes in the collections is immense, not least because this genre has survived the longest as a living tradition; after all, anecdotes are still told today. The Numskull Stories, for example, were very popular and might have been told as a long chain formed from many small episodes. "The numskulls", needless to say, were never representatives of one's own peer groups; these stories were told about the inhabitants of a neighbouring village, tribe or nation. The theme of the clever boy, who deceives the strong but stupid devil time and time again, has also been a great favourite in Finland; this subject category provides ca 100 different tales. These stories about the stupid ogre have been especially popular among young men; a significant number of the narrators are under the age of twenty. The stock characters featured in the humorous tales are the master and his farm-hand, the parson and his assistant, the girl and her suitor, the old maid, the stupid boy and the clever boy, the gypsy, the Russian, etc.

TRADITIONAL CONTEXTS

In the last century, when most of the recorded tales were preserved, storytelling was still a living custom. Stories were told to pass the time whenever people got together and there was a need for entertainment. In winter, the dark evenings in the farm-house were shortened by telling folktales; hunting and fishing trips also provided a convenient opportunity for storytelling by the campfire. The forest work place served as an excellent environment for the oral tradition; the work stations were situated far away from any habitation, men from all over gathered round, and, in the evenings, folktales were almost the only source of entertainment. On trade and market trips, inns and taverns became a meeting place where folk from different regions would congregate. Similarly, during large church festivals, weddings or funerals, one would have an opportunity to hear new, unfamiliar tales, and tell one's own tales to a new audience. Many men report having heard a large number of tales while in military service.

Among the narrators the proportion of men to women was high. Skilled storytellers were often representatives of the itinerant trades: cobblers, tailors, lumberjacks, peddlers and beggars. During the last century it was still common for people of all ages to know folktales. If one surveys large tale collections, such as those of Kaarle Krohn from the 1880s, which comprise around 8000 examples, one discerns that the majority of the narrators fall into the 20- to 40-year-old age group.

Storytelling as a living and active institution gradually ceased to exist in Finland during the nineteenth century. Collectors who travelled in Western Finland in the latter part of the century complain, almost without exception, of the decline and the lack of appreciation of storytelling, despite the fact that a great many tales were recorded, and that there was even a considerable number of young people among the narrators. In Eastern Finland and Karelia the oral tradition continued longer, up to the Second World War in some places.

Naturally, a brief translated selection can only give but a small glimpse of the rich and colourful store of folktales that exist in Finland. The multifaceted beauty of the oral tradition together with the exuberant and vivid use of language by the narrators will inevitably lose a part of its power of expression when transferred to a book, let alone into a foreign language. Nevertheless, I hope that the present edition will, for its own part, awaken interest in the folk culture of a small Nordic country – a folk culture which has played a significant part in the history of that country.

Dr Pirkko-Liisa Rausmaa
Finnish Literature Society

(Translated by Helena Henderson)

Preface

This book is primarily intended as an introduction to the rich oral tradition of Finnish folktales for the English-speaking students of folklore. In this small selection of fifty tales, I have attempted to provide as extensive a range as possible using three different sources as the basis: the vast manuscript collections of the SKS Folklore Archive, Eero Salmelainen's classic collection *Suomen Kansan Satuja ja Tarinoita* (1852–1866) and the current series of folktale publications of the SKS, *Suomalaiset kansansadut* 1–3 (1982–1990), edited by Pirkko-Liisa Rausmaa. My research greatly benefitted from the use of the latter source for its excellent scholarship and comprehensive notes, and indeed, half of my translated selection comes from the Rausmaa editions.

I have sought to include most of the subgroups within the main categories, but by far the largest selection is given to the Ordinary Folktales, the Magic Tales in particular, as these form the most popular division and many types are well-known from the Grimms' versions. Most of the Tale Types in this selection are represented by a single example, with one important exception. The long title story *The Maiden Who Rose From the Sea*, representing the Eastern tradition and which Salmelainen amalgamated from two separate sources, is contrasted with two shorter variants, *The Death of the Wicked Witch* and *The Devoted Orphans*. There is a span of a hundred years between the first and the last recordings.

Translating traditional oral prose narrative imposes particular limitations and challenges. It is naturally impossible to reproduce in translation the variety of regional dialects of the source texts and, therefore, my publisher and I decided early on that I should opt for a literal and neutral style, incorporating some of the colloquialisms and idioms where possible. For the benefit of the general reader, however, I should like to emphasise that for a folklore scholar to be able 'to hear' the voice of the original narrator (warts and all) is of the essence. Therefore, procedures like excessive paraphrasing, changing the style or generally tampering with the original text remain undesirable, albeit occasionally unavoidable. I must admit that this aspect proved perhaps the greatest challenge during my translation—there were times when I found it difficult to refrain from intervening to the point of retelling the stories.

The tales from Salmelainen's collection (Nos 1, 3, 14, 18) deviate from the rest of the tales in their editorial style, which is altogether more formal and literary, characteristic of the Romantic period. I have attempted to reproduce this and have also incorporated the 'historic' present tense, which, again, to a non-specialist might look rather odd in English.

This compilation, although essentially innocent in its narrative, does contain gothic elements and explicit language at times. It might, therefore, be advisable to exercise parental guidance where young children are concerned. I very much hope that this translated collection has at least partly succeeded in recreating the exciting world of Finnish folktales—it has been, for my part, a labour of love.

I am most grateful to the following for their assistance during my work on this anthology: Dr Pirkko-Liisa Rausmaa of Suomalaisen Kirjallisuuden Seura, who so generously gave of her time and expertise during my research in Helsinki both with the selection of the material and textual problems at the translating stage; the Information Centre for Finnish Literature for providing me with a translation grant, and its Director, Marja-Leena Rautalin, for her good-humoured encouragement; Matti Suurpää, Publishing Director of SKS, for kind permission to use SKS publications in copyright; all the staff of the SKS Folklore Archive who could not have been more obliging; Michael Pursglove of the University of Exeter for many useful comments on the translations and advice on some aspects of the vocabulary; Erkki Koivunen for assistance with archaisms and regional dialects; Mike Shields, Editor of *Orbis*, for helpful comments on the verse passages; Irene Alfthan of Amerin Kultuurisäätiö for helping me in my search for the cover illustration; Meri Harmovuori-Jansson and Jarl Jansson for providing me with a peaceful retreat during my research in Helsinki; Alexander and John Henderson for technical support, which enabled me to remain on 'speaking' terms with my computer.

Helena Henderson

The Rabbit, the Wolf, the Fox and the Bear Caught in a Pit

man had dug a pit in the ground and placed a carcass there as bait to lure rabbits, wolves, foxes and bears. And indeed, each of the animals was tempted by the carcass, and all fell into the pit. As they saw no way of escape, the animals felt it best to settle down for a rest.

After a short while they became restless as their hunger returned, one of them asked, "Well, what shall we eat now?" The fox, looking the rabbit over, said, "Let's eat that pop-eyed one first; we're sure to come up with something else later". "Yes, let's eat him", replied the others, and set about eating the rabbit straight away. So they got settled down for another rest and after a while woke up and asked each other, "What shall we eat now to satisfy our hunger?" The fox, while looking at the wolf, said to the others, "Let's eat the hairy one". "Yes, let's do that!" said the others and made fast work of eating the wolf, after which the fox and the bear took another nap.

While the bear was sleeping, the fox got up quietly and placed the wolf's innards under his own belly and went back to sleep. When the bear in turn woke up, he asked the fox, "What shall we eat now? I'm hungry". The fox then scooped up the wolf's innards from under his belly and said, "Gobble up your own innards; I tore my belly open, why don't you do the same?" The bear followed the fox's advice, but as he

1

tore his belly open and began gobbling up his innards, he died there and then. Now the fox, all alone, could eat the bear in peace, and carried on with his life in the pit as best he could.

Eventually the trapper came to the pit to see whether he had caught any prey. The fox then pretended to be dead, and the man, believing this to be so, pulled the fox up and threw him onto the hillside. Mikko* then ran off into the forest and freedom, and thus managed to escape death.

~ ~ ~

The Fox as a Nursemaid

A wolf was looking for a nursemaid. After a while he met a sheep who asked, "Where's the wolf off to?" "I'm looking for a nursemaid". "Take me for your nursemaid", said the sheep.

"Can you sing a pretty lullaby?"

"Baa-aah!" sang the sheep.

"No, you won't do at all, you'll frighten my children", said the wolf.

Then a rabbit came by and asked, "Where's the wolf off to?"

"I'm looking for a nursemaid".

"I'll be your nursemaid".

*A popular name for a fox.

"Can you sing a pretty lullaby?"
"Poo-pooh!" sang the rabbit.

Then a fox came by and asked, "Where's the wolf off to?"

"I'm looking for a nursemaid. Can you sing a pretty lullaby?"

The fox sang a very pretty lullaby and got the job.

The wolf took the fox to his children, and then went to hunt for food. Meanwhile the fox and the children became hungry, so the fox ate the children.

The wolf returned home carrying a sheep on his back and noticed the children had gone. The wolf grabbed hold of the fox between his jaws. The fox asked, "From where does the wind blow when the fox is taken?"

The wolf opened his mouth and answered, "From the west". And the fox leaped out from the wolf's jaws and ran off to the hills singing,

> Tra-la-la there's my trap,
> The wolf cubs in my bag.

The Fox, the Wolf and the Lion

In the olden days, when the animals ruled supreme, it once happened that a lion fell ill, and in that sorry state was unable to watch over his subjects at work, as he had to stay in bed. The cunning fox soon gave up work altogether and just ran about the country, here and there, doing nothing. The wolf was rather annoyed at the fox's behaviour, for he himself would have gladly worked a little less and enjoyed himself on pleasure trips in the forests. Alas, it never occurred to him, fool that he was, to go off without asking. So the wolf took it upon himself to go to the sick lion, and told him about the fox: "That good-for-nothing fox can't be bothered to sit at work, but wanders far and wide".

Hearing this the lion grew very angry and summoned the fox before him and asked, "Why do you run about doing nothing, why aren't you at work as is your duty?"

"Oh, but I have been doing honourable work", whined the fox in protest. "I was searching for medication for a sick lion".

"Well, did you find anything?" asked the muchpleased lion. "Not yet, but I was just about to find something", replied the fox. "I was talking to a spider who lives in the corner of an old barn and he promised to give me some good advice".

"Well, you had better hurry back to the spider for advice; you speak with a silver tongue, maybe you will manage to get something out of him".

The fox went off wandering over hills and dales,

and after travelling for some time he decided to return. "Well, did you manage to obtain any advice?" asked the lion. "I did indeed", replied the fox.

"Well, what kind of advice did the spider give you then?"

"He said", explained the fox, "if we skinned the wolf and placed the skin where it hurts most, you would soon recover". And what do you know, hearing this, the lion had the wolf brought in and had it skinned on the spot. The sly old fox just walked away.

The Dog's Document

In a manor-house there lived a fine old faithful dog, much loved by its master. Once there were two cockrels who were having a fight, and the dog went over to separate them. One of the cockrels died from the dog's bite. This angered the master so much that he drove the dog away from the parish altogether.

The dog then went to hide in a barn, and a wolf happened to come by. "And what creature are you?" asked the wolf. The dog said that he was a cobbler. Hearing this, the wolf said, "Make me some shoes, so that the icy snow wouldn't tear at my feet".

"Well, you'd better go and fetch me a young cow for the leather", said the dog. So the wolf brought the dog a young cow. The dog was enjoying his life, now that he had the young cow to feed on.

The wolf came to see if his shoes were ready yet. "It would be good to have a sheep, so that we could get some cord", said the dog. And the wolf brought a sheep for the dog, and the dog, yet again, could enjoy his life.

When the wolf called in again to see if his shoes were ready, the dog told him, "You should bring me a pig, so that I could get some ointment". When the pig was brought over, the dog once more was enjoying a good life.

When the wolf called again to see if his shoes were ready, the dog growled angrily at the wolf and said, "Let's have a battle; go and gather as many wolves as I'll have dogs". But the wolf didn't manage to recruit as many wolves as the dog had dogs. So they fought the battle in the field, and the dog drove all the wolves from the whole parish so that there was not a single wolf left.

Now the dog went to court to ask for maintenance as a reward for having driven the wolves out of the parish. The court then furnished the dog with a document which stated that one should feed dogs. One day they stopped at the Roumu* house and wanted to take some food with them, but were told that feeding dogs was not compulsory. So the dog looked for the document which the house-cat had put away on the top of the fireplace where the mice had torn it to pieces. Only one piece of the paper was found—the piece where it stated that dogs should be fed. The dogs then gathered at the beach, and when they went for a swim the document was

*A proper name.

placed under the tail of one of the dogs; a solid bushy tail it was, too. They swam off from the Roumu house and when they arrived at the next house, the dogs began sniffing each other's tails to find where the document was so that they could be fed, but the document had been lost in the stream.

Ever since then when two dogs meet they still sniff under each other's tails. And that is why the dog is angry with the cat, and the cat with the mice.

The Pig and the Squirrel

One autumn morning the pig happened to meet the squirrel in the forest, by the turnip-field enclosure. After they thought for a moment what to say to each other, the squirrel finally said, "You fool; although you're a whole fathom taller than everyone else, I can see the sun rise before you!"

"What nonsense you are babbling, you ragamuffin", said the pig. "I'll bet as much as you like on it!"

"It's all the same to me—the turnip-field will be the wager!" said the squirrel. "All right, let's do that. Let's shake hands on it!" replied the pig. Then the squirrel struck the pig's hand so hard that the tip of the pig's hand—which until then had been in one piece—split in two, because the squirrel's nail had cut it so deeply. Since then all the pig's trotters have been split into two.

The squirrel then climbed up right to the top of a tall spruce, and turned his head towards the east, in order to watch the sun rise. The pig placed his snout on a fallen tree trunk which lay at the bottom of the spruce, and directed its snout towards the west. Every now and then he would mutter, "Oink, oink!"

Eventually, when the rosy hue coloured the blue skies in the west, the pig said, "Well, well, now the sun is rising!" The squirrel had not yet spotted the sun rise; and therefore, had to confess that the pig had won the bet. The pig, overjoyed with his win, went over to the turnip-field and enjoyed feasting on the turnips and became so fond of that eating place that he didn't want to move away until the autumn, when the turnips had been harvested.

The Wedding Roast

Preparations for a wedding were under way in the house and as there wasn't any roast yet, the farm-hand asked his master, "Where can we get a roast for the wedding, sir?" "Well, there's a bull in the cowshed, isn't there?" replied the master.

A cat which was sitting on top of the oven overheard this and rushed over to the bull in order to warn him. "You'd better get going fast; otherwise you'll end up on the table as the wedding roast!" So the bull went to the woods.

When the farm-hand went into the cattleshed there was no sign of the bull there. The farm-hand went back into the farmhouse kitchen and said to his master, "There was no bull there; where do we get the wedding roast from?"

"Well, the goat is sure to be in the cattleshed", replied his master.

When the cat overheard this, he went over to the goat. "Run to the forest straight away, otherwise they'll make the wedding roast out of you!"

When the farm-hand went into the cattleshed he couldn't see the goat. So he went over to his master and told him, "There was no goat in the cattleshed; where do we get the wedding roast from now?"

"Well, there's a stallion in the stable", replied the master.

Overhearing this, the cat rushed over to the stallion saying, "Run to the woods quickly or you'll be the roast for the wedding!" The stallion did as he was told.

When the farm-hand went to the stable he saw that even the stallion had disappeared, and went over to his master and said, "There was no stallion in the stable. Where do we get the wedding roast from now?"

"Well, at least there must be a cockrel roosting", replied the master.

Hearing this, the cat went over to the cockrel and said, "Quickly, go to the woods, or they'll make the wedding roast out of you!" And the cockrel went to the woods.

When the farm-hand couldn't find the cockrel roosting, he said to his master, "Where, now, do we get the wedding roast from, as there was no cockrel roosting?"

Finally, the master got very angry and bellowed, "There's a cat on top of the oven!" When the cat heard this, it got very frightened and jumped out of the window into the yard and ran off into the woods; so it joined the bull, the goat, the stallion and the cockrel, and they were later joined by a bear, a fox and a hare.

When the night came, the cat went to a house to ask for a night's lodgings, but was told, "There is no other room except the lonely barn. A gnome wanders about there every night".

"That's not dangerous; we'll go there", replied the cat. And so, they all settled in—the fox in the fireplace, the cat on top of the oven, the bear and the stallion at the back of the room, the hare in the corner, the goat on the floor, the bull by the doorway, and the cockrel went to roost on the porch.

At midnight the gnome came into the room and went to take a splint from the oven and some matches from the top of the oven. But when he took the splint the fox scratched his eye, and when he took the matches the cat scratched his other eye. The gnome escaped to the floor, but the goat butted him right to the back of the room, where the bear and the stallion nearly tore him to pieces and threw him to the doorway, where the bull, with his horns, butted him out through the porch, while the cockrel was singing at his roost in the porch.

The gnome, barely alive, went to the other gnomes and told them, "When I took some matches from the top of the oven they took my eye out, and when I reached for a splint they took my other eye. When I went into the middle of the floor, I was hit in the back with a fist so hard that I fell to the back of the room. There my older brother beat me up and threw me to the doorway. In the doorway some old man threw me out with a pitchfork into the yard. And someone on the porch kept shouting: "Hit and butt, hit and butt!"

The Reward of the Benefactor

While walking in the woods, a hunter spotted a rock which had cracked. A snake had fallen into the stony crevice and, realising that he would not be able to get out by himself, asked the hunter for help. This the hunter did, but when he demanded his reward, the snake said, "I'm going to eat you now, for death is the usual reward for the benefactor". The hunter was not pleased with this verdict and said, "The first animal we come across shall be the judge of this".

After walking a short while they met a dog. The hunter told the dog about the business, and asked for the animal's decision in the matter. The dog replied, "I've served my master for eight years, in which time I've barked and driven away the good and the bad alike, but this is where I've been brought to die". The man wasn't satisfied with this verdict either and said, "Now the next animal we come across shall be our judge".

After a short while they met a fox. The hunter again explained his business, and asked the fox to pass the correct judgement. The fox told the man to take the snake to the same stony crevice where he had rescued the snake. The snake was taken and placed in the crevice, the fox passed his sentence, "There he wriggles—cover him with stones!" The man did as he was told and stoned the snake to death.

Now it was the fox's turn to demand a reward. "I have thirty hens in my hen-house; go and help yourself to as many as your belly will take", replied the man. The hunter rushed home and said to his son, "If you want to catch a fox, now's the time to go and lay in wait".

In the night when the fox came for his supper, the boy shot the fox. And so, the benefactor was rewarded with death, yet again.

Aal, Taal and Everaal

n a small cottage in the woods there once lived a brother and a sister, and they had three sheep. But soon they ran out of food, and the sister said to her brother, "You'd better go and sell one of those sheep so that we can buy something to eat".

The boy set off with one of the sheep. They met a grey old man with a stick in his hand, who said, "Sell me that sheep of yours; I'll give you this dog".

"No, I won't sell it; what good is a dog to me when I need food?"

"Well, I'll give you some money also. The dog is called Aal and it will follow you if you call to it, 'Aal, follow me!'"

The boy agreed to the sale. Now that he had some money, he returned home with his dog. His sister said, "You fool, you've exchanged a sheep for a dog; you have been really foolish! What will you do with a dog, when there's nothing to eat!"

"But surely we need a dog as well", said the boy, "and I was also paid a sum of money, so we can buy bread".

After a while they ran out of bread, and the girl said to her brother, "Go and sell another sheep, so that we will not starve".

Well, the boy went off again and met the same grey old man with a stick in his hand and said, "Sell me your sheep; I'll give you a dog!"

"No, I won't; what would I do with so many dogs, when I already have one? My sister will reproach me, as there's no bread".

"I'll give you some money as well", said the man. Well, the boy took the dog, and the old man said, "This dog is called Taal".

The boy went home with the dog, and his sister said, "You haven't exchanged another sheep for a dog, have you? What on earth do you think you're doing? It's food we need". The boy said, "Don't you fret; I also have some money for bread".

But after a while they ran out of bread again. How could it last any longer, with such little money! The girl said to the boy, "Go and get some bread for us now. You'll have to sell our last sheep, but on no account exchange it for another dog".

The boy set off with the sheep on his shoulders. The same old grey man came by and said, "Let me have that sheep of yours; I'll give you a dog for it".

"No way, I don't want any more dogs", said the boy. "I already have two of them".

"Just take this one; you won't regret it. They'll do whatever you ask of them, and I'll give you the price of a sheep. This dog is called Everaal, and it will do whatever you want".

Well, the boy went home, and his sister was astonished. "What fine things are you planning to do with these dogs? We can't even feed them. You really are a proper fool! Perhaps you're planning to go hunting with them?"

"Yes", replied the boy.

The boy then went to the woods and told his dogs to come with him. He saw an elk and said, "Aal, Taal and Everaal, catch that elk for me!" They soon caught it and brought it home just as the boy had ordered them. So now there was elk-meat and they got a good price for the skin.

Now the girl said, "They do seem to be very good

dogs. We must feed them really well".

The boy then went to the woods again and saw a bear. He told his dogs to kill the bear. The dogs killed the bear and took it home, as the boy had told them to, and again there was money and food. And the girl no longer complained that her brother had exchanged the sheep for the dogs.

With the help from his dogs, the boy became very rich. Once some thieves stopped by to ask for a bed for the night, but the boy wouldn't let them stay as he knew what kind of men they were. They then tried to force their way in through the door. The boy said, "Aal, hold the door!"

Aal took hold of the door, so that the thieves couldn't get in. They tried another door, but the boy said, "Taal, get hold of that door!"

Taal held the door so that they couldn't get in through there, either. They then tried to get in through the window. But the boy said, "Everaal, get them!" Everaal pounced on the thieves, tore them to pieces, removed the money from their pockets and took it to the boy who now had great riches.

One day the boy was walking with his dogs in the forest and there he saw the king's footman crying. The boy said, "What's troubling you and what are you looking for here?"

"The evil one will take the king's daughter, as there is no man strong enough to save her. I'm here to take the spruce of sorrow to the palace".

"Don't worry at all", said the boy. "I will come tomorrow with my dogs". The princess was expected to be given in the meadow the next day.

The following day the boy went with his dogs to the meadow, where the princess was now waiting. In the crack-willow a man was hiding, holding the hatchet which he would use to fight the evil one. The princess was deep in sorrow but the boy consoled her, "Don't be sad; I'll frighten the evil one with my dogs!" The princess said, "It will cough three times when it's approaching: the first time it will cough from three leagues away, the second time from two leagues away and when it coughs the third time, it's only one league away; then it will come, the evil one, and take me away!" But the boy replied, "Don't worry at all. I'll just go and rest for a little while".

Then the evil one coughed for the first time, and the princess began pleading with the boy to help her. The hatchet-man was supposed to come down from the tree to help, but didn't as he was so frightened. But the boy just kept on sleeping. The evil one then coughed for the second time, which meant that it was already within two leagues. The princess tried again to wake the boy and ask for his help, but the boy wouldn't be roused, which made the princess cry. The evil one coughed for the third time, and that's when the princess began sobbing dreadfully and pleaded with the boy, but he just continued to sleep soundly. It wasn't until the evil one pushed the princess to the ground that the boy got up and said, "Aal, dig your claws into him!" And Aal ravaged the enemy so badly that it begged, "Leave me with some breath at least!"

"Do you promise not to come a second time?" asked the boy. "Will you now keep away from here?"

"Yes, yes, I promise!" said the evil one, but as it was leaving, added, "I shall be back two more times!"

The boy set off for home and said, "I'll be back tomorrow for the second return". The evil one was due to return every day for the next three days.

The boy and his dogs returned to the meadow on the next day. The princess was still in the meadow, and the man with his hatchet was still in the crackwillow. When the evil one arrived the second time, it made a much greater noise, and the princess was in great distress. The boy got up and said, "Taal, attack!" The dog savaged the evil one so badly that it began begging for mercy and said, "Leave me with a little life intact, please, just a little bit!"

"Will you not come back again", asked the boy, "if I let you go in peace?"

"No, I'll not return any more", said the enemy, "if I get out of here in one piece!" And again it said, when leaving, "But I will be back tomorrow". The man in the crack-willow was trembling with fear and dared not come down.

The boy then left for home, but promised to come back with his dogs on the third day. The evil one returned in its very worst and most evil form—the man in the crack-willow even dropped his hatchet—and its cough was louder than ever. The boy was sleeping again, and the princess was in great distress, as she thought that now even the boy with his dogs would be unable to protect her, and pleaded with the boy to wake up, in order to defend her. But the boy didn't get up until the evil one had attacked the princess.

"Everaal", called the boy, "attack!" Everaal attacked ferociously, and the evil one was now in a worse state than ever. It began praying for mercy and said, "At least leave me with some sign of life! I shall not come back again, never ever again!"

The boy ordered Everaal to stop the attack. Everaal stopped, and the evil one shuffled on its way and mumbled to itself, "I shall never come back, I shall never come back! Everaal was always the best dog! Everaal's the best, Everaal's the best!"

The princess had been saved, and the boy went home instead of going to the king's castle. The princess had invited him there, as she had been promised in marriage to the one who would save her. But the boy had just left for home. Now the other man came down from the crack-willow and made the princess swear that he was the one who had saved her, and threatened to kill her if she refused. Well, what else could the princess do but give her word?

When the princess and the hatchet-man arrived at the castle, it had been draped in black mourning, since they believed that the evil one had already taken the princess away forever. But now everyone was filled with great joy and wished to know how the princess had managed to escape. "I saved her with this hatchet!" exclaimed the man. "So he did", attested the princess.

Well, the man was promised the princess in marriage, and they had their banns called in church the following Sunday. The boy was at the church and thought to himself, "How can this be, when the princess was promised to the one who saved her?"

The boy went to the castle and took his dogs with him. The bridegroom saw the boy sitting on the balcony, and then asked the king for permission to sit behind three locked doors. "What's the matter with the bridegroom?" asked the king. "I'm very frightened of those dogs", he answered. "They won't harm you", said the king. "But I'm still frightened of them just the same", said the bridegroom. The bridegroom was put behind three locked doors.

The boy went to the first door and said, "Aal, open this door!" Aal pounced on the door and opened it. There was another door, stronger than the first, and the boy said, "Taal, open the door!" Taal flung the door open. After that there was a heavy iron door, and the boy said, "Aal, open the door!" Aal tried but couldn't get it open. "Taal, open the door!" Taal rushed towards the door, but it wouldn't open as it was so heavy.

"Everaal, your turn to try!" And Everaal pulled so hard that even the hinges rattled, and the boy said to the bridegroom, "Don't even try getting away from me; you won't be able to, however much you try!" And the boy made him confess everything.

On the wedding day the boy arrived with his dogs. A magnificent wedding table was laid, and the boy called, "Aal, go and push the table over!" Aal went and turned everything upside down.

This was met with great disapproval and everyone wondered why the boy had brought such dogs to the wedding. Another table was laid, more beautiful and handsome than the first. The boy said, "Taal, turn the table upside down!" and Taal wrecked the table.

The guests were saying that one shouldn't have such awful dogs and that their owner should be sued as he was responsible for their behaviour. Then an even more festive table was laid, and the guests began to eat, but the boy said, "Go, Everaal, go!" Everaal went and began slapping the guests on their cheeks with legs of pork. Even the king ran for cover behind many locked doors, but the boy and his dogs went everywhere, and eventually, the princess confessed that it was the boy who, along with his dogs, had saved her from the evil one.

A wedding banquet was held for the boy and the

princess. The hatchet-man was executed with the hatchet he had carried while hiding in the tree. The boy's sister became a lady-in-waiting and she no longer had to live in their small cottage in the woods. After this the sister would always say that the dogs had brought them so much good fortune, which the sheep wouldn't have been able to. The dogs were kept with the army to protect the kingdom.

I left after I had some porridge at the wedding.

The Three Missing Princesses

Once the king's wife gave birth to triplets. Sages were brought in to tell what the future had in store for the princesses— whether good or evil. One of them said, "If the daughters are allowed out before their fifteenth birthday, they will encounter evil; they will vanish".

Their fifteenth birthday was approaching, and it was a hot summer's day. They wished to be in the garden, and so were let out into the small herb garden, and three soldiers with swords in their hands were there to guard them. But, nevertheless, the daughters disappeared from the herb garden. The king said that whoever could find them would receive half the kingdom together with one of his daughters for a wife. The whole world searched for them but could not find them.

The king had a stableboy who then said, "Let me

go and search for them!" The king said, "And how do you think you could find them, when even your betters haven't been able to?" The boy said, "Be that as it may, let me at least try". He put his small axe on his shoulder and went to look for the princesses.

On the road he met on old man who had iron teeth and iron fingernails. The boy took such a fright that he hit his axe on a log which was lying by the road, and the log split and the axe got stuck in the crack. The boy began to plead with the old man, "Put your fingernail into the crack and break the wood in half, so that I can remove my axe!" The old man did this, and the boy gave a heave and got his axe out. Then the old man pleaded, "Strike with your axe, so that I may get my nail out!"

"No, I won't, unless you tell me where the three king's daughters are!" The old man said, "One is in a pit one hundred fathoms deep, the second in a pit two hundred fathoms deep, and the third in a pit as deep as three hundred fathoms".

But the boy still wouldn't free him, but asked how he could get the daughters out. The old man gave him a whistle and said, "Whenever you blow this whistle, I will come straight away". So the boy set him free.

Then the boy went to the pit that was a hundred fathoms deep and blew the whistle. The old man appeared. "What does the young man wish?"

"Nothing much, but tell me how to get this girl out of the pit?"

"I'll lower you down with a rope", said the old man, and added, "There you'll find a bottle of water; when you drink it, you'll become stronger than anybody. On the wall you'll find the sword of Solomon, and with that sword you'll defeat the devil whose head the girl is looking after".

The old man lowered the boy down with the rope, and there was one of the king's daughters in an iron cage, with an iron crown on her head and an iron ring on her finger. She was looking at the devil's head which was asleep on her lap. The girl said, "How did you get here, my young man? When this old devil wakes up, he'll eat you!" The boy said, "No fear of that!"

The devil woke up and said, "Phew, is it the blood of a Christian that stinks the place out?" The boy drank the water of strength and snatched the sword of Solomon from the wall and cut the devil's head off. Then he blew his whistle. The old man came and asked, "What does the young man wish?"

"Nothing much, but now I'd need to get down a two hundred fathom pit".

The old man lowered the boy down again and said, "The bottle of strength-water is on the window sill, and the sword of Solomon is hanging on the wall".

The boy drank the power-giving water. Then a girl, wearing a silver crown in a silver cage with a silver ring on her finger, was looking after a two-headed devil. She said, "Where did you come from, my young man? When this one wakes up, he'll eat you up!" "No fear of that!" said the lad.

The devil woke up and said, "Ooh, Christian blood really does stink!" The boy again snatched Solomon's sword from the wall and cut the heads off. The boy blew the whistle once more, and the old man came. "What does the young man wish?"

"Well, nothing really, but how does one get down a three hundred fathom pit?"

"I'll lower you down with a rope. Again you'll

find a bottle by the window; take a swig and you'll be stronger than anybody. And the sword of Solomon hangs on the wall; if you're strong enough to lift it you'll be able to kill the devil. In another bottle you'll find water; when you drink it, you'll become healthy, no matter how badly you may have been injured".

The old man lowered the boy down. There was a girl in a golden cage wearing a crown of gold, with a golden ring on her finger. She was watching over a three-headed devil, and said, "How did you manage to get down here, my young man? When this one here wakes up, he'll kill you". "No fear of that", said the boy. He took a drink of the water and tried lifting the sword but failed. He then finished the bottle, snatched the sword of Solomon and cut all the heads off.

He then picked up the cages, the crowns and the rings and put them all into a sack and blew the whistle. The old man came, "What does the young man wish?"

"Nothing else, just tell me how to get everything out of here?"

"I'll use the rope", said the old man, "but I'll pull the daughters up first, and you'll come after them with your sack of goods".

Some soldiers were guarding the mouth of the pit. After the king's daughters had been pulled out of the pit, the soldiers cut through the rope. The boy fell three hundred fathoms down the pit with his sack and was nearly killed. However, he managed to revive himself and remembered what the old man had said about the other bottle of water. He took a swig from the bottle and became healthier than he'd ever been. He then blew the whistle and the old man came: "What does the young man wish?"

"Nothing, but how does one get out of here?"

"I'll pull you up with the rope".

Now the boy was back on the surface, but he didn't dare follow the soldiers because he feared they would kill him. The soldiers had taken the king's daughters back to the castle and claimed that they had found them. The boy then went to serve as a blacksmith's apprentice and buried his sack at the back of the workshop.

A short time passed, and the king made a decree, stating that whoever was able to make an iron cage, an iron crown and an iron ring exactly like those his daughter had in the mountain crevice, would have her for his wife and half of his kingdom. The blacksmith tried his hand at this, but towards the evening his apprentice said, "Master, let me have a try". The blacksmith said, "How would you be able to, since I couldn't?" The boy was busy all night. At the back of the workshop there was a sack from which he took an iron cage, an iron crown and an iron ring and, in the morning, took them to the blacksmith, saying, "Master, take these things and say you made them yourself!"

The blacksmith thought this was a good idea. The king and the blacksmith were planning to kill his old wife, so he would be able to marry the king's daughter and receive a large estate.

Soon after, a message arrived stating that whoever could make a silver cage, a silver crown and a silver ring like the ones the king's other daughter had in the crevice, would get her hand in marriage and half the kingdom. The blacksmith spent the whole day in trying make these things. In the evening the boy said, "Master, let me try and make them". "How

would you be able to, when even I can't?", he
answered. The boy went to work in the night and
took a silver cage, a silver crown and a silver ring
from the sack and took them to the blacksmith in the
morning. He told the blacksmith to take them to the
king and say it was his own work. The blacksmith,
thinking this a good idea, did as the boy had
suggested.

Then a message arrived again saying that whoever
was able to make a golden cage, a golden crown and a
golden ring exactly like the ones the king's daughter
had had in the crevice, would get the girl and half
the kingdom. Again the blacksmith tried, but did not
succeed. At nightfall the apprentice went to work
yet again, but suddenly the old man with iron teeth
and iron fingernails appeared without a blow on
the whistle and said, "Don't do anything now. The
blacksmith is keeping a watch and will kill you if he
sees you!"

So the boy just slept in the workshop and, in the
morning, told his master that nothing had come out
of it. The blacksmith spent the whole day working
very hard, but was unable to produce anything. The
following night, while the blacksmith was asleep, the
boy tried again and got the crown and the ring ready.
After making the cage the boy blew his whistle, and
the old man appeared and asked, "What does the
young man wish?"

"Nothing else, but I wish I could have a golden
carriage with golden horses and clothes of gold, so
that I may drive to the king!"

And there they were—the golden horses with
the golden carriage and the clothes of gold, and all
the while the blacksmith just kept sleeping. Without
delay the boy set off. The soldiers were watching and

waiting for the blacksmith to arrive; they planned to kill him and take the crown to the king themselves. But instead, the soldiers who were standing by the side of the road could do nothing but bow in respect when the carriage whistled past them. They had no idea that it was the bringer of the golden cage, the golden crown and the golden ring.

The boy then drove into the king's castle, and a big wedding banquet was held. And that's the end of that.

The Three Brothers

There was a husband and a wife, and the husband had grown so lazy that he did nothing at all. The wife had to feed and look after him, and had become thoroughly fed up with the situation. She went out visiting and told the others there just how lazy her husband was, and wondered what she could do with him. Her neighbours advised her to cook some very salty food and serve it to him. Then she should take all the water away from the farmhouse and go on a visit herself, so the man would then be forced to go and get some water himself.

The woman did as she had been advised and then went out visiting. The man became very thirsty, and remembering there was a river nearby, went out for a drink. The man had put on a lot of weight from lolling in bed for so long, but apart from that he was healthy—healthy and lazy; however, he could no longer bend down to drink from the river. He had to wade into a deeper part of the river until the water ran straight into his mouth. Just then a perch swam into his mouth. The man held the fish between his teeth, and the perch said, "Don't kill me! Let me go, wade a bit deeper and you'll get a large pike!"

The man let the perch go and waded deeper. Then a pike swam into his mouth, and a very big one at that. The man took the pike home and cooked some fresh fish soup, enough to serve his wife. When she came home, the man told her how he'd caught the fish. As they ate the fish, the man said they should save the pike's bones, "In case they'll be needed one day".

Then, suddenly, plenty of work came the man's way. On the first night his wife gave birth to three sons. When the man went to check the dog kennel, the bitch had had three puppies. Then he went to the stable, and the horse had had three foals.

The boys began to grow so vigorously that at fourteen days, they were already as big and strong as other boys at the age of fourteen years. The father went to the school to enrol his sons and said they were fourteen days old. The teacher asked, "What do they want with school, such young boys?" But the father said, "Oh, they're already as big as other boys of fourteen years".

The boys were admitted to the school. There were also three king's sons at the school who liked to play with a rubber ball during break time. The old man's sons had nothing to play with. The boys told their father that they also needed a ball that they could throw around, so the father made them a wooden ball. The boys took it with them to school and were throwing the ball about, and the king's sons went to play with them. It so happened that a wooden ball struck the eldest king's son on the head, which made him say wicked things. One of the old man's boys got hold of the king's son by his hair and twisted his neck until it broke, and the king's son died.

The next day the boys went out again to play ball. Now the second king's son was hit on the head and he, too, began to say wicked things. The old man's son got hold of the king's son's nose and twisted his neck until it broke.

The king was sent a message explaining what had happened to his sons. The king thought that there was nothing he could do with these boys as they were so young, they couldn't really be punished, and ordered that his youngest son must not be allowed to play with them. But the son got out secretly, and the same thing happened to him.

The king wanted to see what these boys were like and sent his army to fetch them. The boys had weapons made from pike's bones, and destroyed the army. The king promptly sent out a second army to fetch the boys, but they destroyed this army as well.

The king told them to leave the kingdom altogether. The boys promised to leave, if they'd get one thousand marks* and a good horse each. They were each given the money and the horses. But when they stroked the horses, the animals collapsed in front of them. They then asked for more money and promised to leave, taking their own horses instead.

The brothers were given the money and left. They

Markka: The former Finnish unit of currency.

came to a crossroads where the road forked out in three directions. Each boy went his separate way, leaving his own sign at the crossroads. Should any of them encounter danger, the sign would be affected, and if one of the brothers should return to that same place, he would go to help the one whose sign was marred. They then went their separate ways, and each had a dog and a horse, which their father had given them.

On his journey, the eldest brother happened to come to a king's castle, and was immediately taken into the king's court as a son-in-law. In the evening he was looking out of the window and saw a fire blazing in the backwoods. He asked the king's daughter, "What is that fire in the distance?"

"Nobody knows that", said the king's daughter.

"I'll go and have a look", said the boy.

"It's not a good idea to go there", said the king's daughter. "Many have ventured there but nobody has ever returned".

"Well, perhaps I shan't go there, after all", said the boy.

But when the king's daughter was asleep, the boy slipped out with his horse and his dog. When he had reached the bonfire, an old crone came from the backwoods and said, "Brr, how cold it is!"

"There's a fire over here", said the boy. "Come and warm yourself up!"

"I dare not", said the old crone. "Your dog will bite and your horse will kick. Take a strand of hair from your head and with it, tie them up to a tree!" The boy did as the old crone told him, and at that very moment, they—the horse, the dog and the boy—all turned to stone.

The second brother came to the crossroads and

saw that there was something wrong with the eldest brother's sign. He followed the same road and came to the same king's castle, where they thought him to be the son-in-law, as the brothers looked so alike.

In the evening he saw the same fire glowing in the backwoods, and asked the king's daughter, "What is that fire burning in the distance?"

"But I already told you yesterday", said the king's daughter, "that nobody knows anything about that fire".

"I'll go and have a look", said the boy.

"It's not good to go there", said the king's daughter. "Many have ventured there but none has ever returned".

"Well, I shan't go there then", said the boy.

But all the same, he went as soon as the king's daughter was asleep. The same old crone came from the backwoods and said, "Oooh, how cold it is!"

"There's a fire over here; come and get warm", said the boy.

"I daren't", said the old crone. "Your dog will bite and your horse will kick me. Take a strand of hair from your head and tie them with it!" The boy did as the old woman had told him, and turned to stone along with his horse and his dog.

The youngest brother then came to the crossroads and, seeing that both of his brothers' signs were faulty, he thought, "I suppose my other brother went to the rescue of the eldest one, and now they both have met with misfortune".

He travelled down the road and came to the same king's castle, and again, the castle folk thought that he, too, was one and the same boy. In the evening he spotted the same flames in the backwoods and asked the king's daughter, "What is that fire over there?"

"But I have told you twice already, nobody knows anything about it".

"I'll go and see for myself", said the boy.

"It's not good to go there", said the king's daughter. "Many have ventured there, but so far none has returned".

The boy noticed that this was where his other brothers had gone. When the king's daughter was asleep, he went to the fire taking his horse and his dog with him. Again the same old crone came from the backwoods and said, "Oooh, how cold it is!"

"There's a fire over here; come and get warm", said the boy.

"I daren't", said the old crone. "Your dog will bite and your horse will kick. Take a strand of hair from your head and with it, tie them to the tree!"

But the boy didn't. Being that much the wiser than his brothers, he had already guessed what the problem was, and kept insisting that the old crone came over to warm up by the fire. But the old crone wouldn't come. The boy told his dog to fetch her, but the dog couldn't manage it by himself. The boy told his horse to go and help and so, together they managed to bring the crone to the fire. There the boy tormented her until she confessed what had happened to the brothers, the horses and the dogs. The old crone had no intention of telling the boy anything but as he wouldn't let go, she had to reveal her secret. She said that under a tree stump there was a bottle, and from that bottle one had to pour three drops on every stump. The boy took the bottle and poured the drops on the stumps, and everyone came back to life again.

The second brother said, "I slept next to your wife last night!" The eldest brother got very angry and, pulling his sword from the sheath, chopped the second brother's head off. The youngest brother began to scold him. "How could you do this, just as I've brought you all back to life again, and now you've gone and killed again".

Now they were in a fix—how to attach the head back on the body? The brothers began bothering the old crone again and wouldn't give up until she gave them the advice, "Over there under that stump there's another bottle. If you pour three drops, the person will become his old self again".

They took the bottle and did as she had advised. But they accidently put the head on back to front, so that the eyes were on the back. They had to cut the head off again and secure it properly.

After this the brothers turned to the old crone once more. They pestered her until they were able to squeeze out the knowledge for bringing all the people, who were on the ground as stones and stumps, back to life again. The old crone didn't want to say but as the brothers wouldn't relent, she had no choice and told them that there was yet another bottle under the stump. When you poured three drops onto every stone and stump, they would all rise up. The boys did just as the crone had advised, and a terrifically large crowd of people rose up.

They roasted the old crone, she was all burnt except for her heart. Finally, even the heart burst in half and the entire back woods was freed from witchcraft.

All the boys went back to the king's castle, and the eldest brother was allowed to keep the king's daughter.

Three Brothers Caught by the Devil

There were three brothers; one was stupid and the other two were clever. One day they went to the forest and came to a clearing. It happened to be the devil's plot of land, and some turnips had been planted there which now had grown ripe enough to be eaten. The boys stopped there and began to eat the turnips. But as they were eating, the devil came over and built a stone wall around the plot so high that the boys were unable to get out.

The clever boys grew very worried, but the stupid boy was in no hurry at all; he just sat there amongst the turnips and ate with great relish. Eventually, the devil returned and took all the boys to his home, where he had three daughters. The devil was going out and said to his daughters, "Roast these boys in the oven for my return".

When the devil had left, the eldest daughter came and asked, "Which one of you boys will be the first to go into the oven?"

"I'll go first", said the stupid boy.

The boy climbed onto the trolley, which was used for shoving food into the oven, and sat down in an awkward position. The devil's daughter said, "That's not how you should sit, you fool!" But the boy answered, "I don't know how to sit here; come and show me how to do it properly".

The daughter took her clothes off and sat on the trolley. But the boy shoved her into the oven. There the daughter began bawling and howling and asked the boy to let her out, but the stupid boy said, "Oh no, I won't let you out!"

The daughter then died in the oven, and when she was well roasted, the boy took her out of the oven, and then to the devil's barn.

After that the second daughter came and asked the two clever boys, "Which one of you will go into the oven first?" The braver of the two answered, "I will!"

And when the daughter told him to sit on the trolley, the boy lay down awkwardly. The daughter said, "Oh, you silly fool, that's not the way you should be sitting!"

"I don't think I can sit any better; why don't you come and show me first how it should be done!"

The girl took her clothes off and showed him how to sit on the trolley. But then the boy pushed her into the oven. The daughter began to cry dreadfully and asked the boy to let her out, but the boy said, "I'll do no such thing!" He left the daughter in the oven long enough for her to get well cooked and then took her out into the devil's barn where the eldest daughter had also been taken.

Then the youngest daughter came and told the other clever boy to sit on the trolley, but the boy went on all fours. The girl said, "That's not how to sit there; you are sitting like a right fool!"

"I shan't be able to sit here any better, until you show me first how it should be done", replied the boy.

The daughter got undressed and sat on the trolley. The boy shoved her into the oven straight away. The girl began calling the devil for help, and promised to give the boy as much gold and silver as he was able to carry, only if he were to let her out of the oven.

But the boy laughed and said, "Oh no, I shan't let you go!" and left the poor girl in the oven until she was well done, then took her out of the oven and then to the barn to join her sisters.

Now that the daughters were all cooked, the boys put on the girls' clothes and their earrings. The devil then returned home and thought the boys to be his daughters and said, "Well, have you cooked the boys yet?" The stupid boy answered, "Yes, we have". The devil said, "Bring me the scales and I'll see how much they weigh".

The stupid boy brought the scales and went into the barn with the devil. When the devil looked his cooked daughters over, he said, "Hasn't that one got fingers just like my daughter's!" Just then the stupid boy took the scales and struck the devil on his forehead so hard that he died.

Now that all the devil's folk were dead, the clever boys said, "Let's get out of here quickly!" But the stupid boy said, "Not so fast; first we have to make a coffin for the devil". Even the clever boys agreed to this, and the coffin was made. After that the boys were ready to leave. But the stupid boy said, "Let's take the coffin with the devil inside along with us!" The clever boys answered, "We can't be bothered to carry it, but if you're willing to do it by yourself, then go ahead!" The stupid boy said, "I don't mind carrying it!"

So the boys left the dead devil's house. The stupid boy carried the coffin with the devil's remains on his back. When the night drew closer, the clever boys said, "We daren't spend the night on the ground; let's climb up the tree for the night, as there are many robbers nearby". The stupid boy said, "Let's do that!" And the boys all climbed up the tree, but then the stupid one said, "I'll take this coffin up with me". The clever boys said, "Don't bother; hide it in the ground". But the stupid boy said, "No, I'll take it, come what may!"

The clever boys agreed on the condition that he should hold on to the coffin all night long. The stupid boy said, "I'll hold on to it". And so the coffin was pulled up the tree.

When they had sat up there a while, the stupid boy said to the others, "The robbers are coming!" Indeed, a great band of robbers had arrived and stopped under the very tree where the boys were hiding. The robbers made a campfire under the tree and began to cook some porridge. They had plenty of valuable treasure: gold, silver and other precious items. The stupid boy said, "This coffin is far too heavy for me to hold. I'm going to drop it!" The clever boy said, "Don't, brother dear, drop it! We'll help you hold on to it, because if you drop it, the robbers will notice us. They'll come and get us, and then we'll be in their clutches". But the stupid boy said, "But I'm about to drop it!" And right then he dropped the coffin down from the tree.

As the coffin fell, its lid opened up, and the devil's corpse fell straight into the the robbers' porridge. When the robbers saw that, they got such a fright that they fled as fast as they could. The boys climbed down from the tree and divided the robbers' treasure amongst themselves.

And that is how the boys became rich men.

The Smith and the Devil

O nce there was a smith to whom I came to do some forging. One day, when we were in the workshop, the smith began to moan about his poverty. After he had talked a while, the devil came up to the door of the workshop and said, "I know why you're so miserable, smith!"

"And how would you know?" asked the smith.

"Because you're as poor as a church mouse. But if you promise to give yourself to me, you will become a very rich man indeed, and you'll never be short of money however much you spend", replied the devil.

The smith agreed to this and asked when he should come to join the devil. The devil said, "I will come back in a year's time; be ready to go with me".

When nearly a year had passed, and the day for leaving was approaching, Saint Peter came to the workshop and asked the smith to shoe his horse. The smith said he hadn't the time to do it as he had to go to join the devil soon. Then Saint Peter said, "If you shoe my horse, I'll give you such power that when the devil comes back to the workshop, whatever he'll touch he'll become stuck to, as though he were nailed down".

The smith complied with Peter's wishes, shod his horse and then began forging a sickle. Just then the devil arrived in a big carriage in front of the workshop and asked the smith to get on board.

"Please step into my workshop and wait a little, while I make this sickle. I'll be ready to go straight after", said the smith.

The devil went into the workshop and stood leaning against the vice. When the smith had finished the sickle, he said to the devil, "Let's go then!"

The devil struggled all he could to remove himself from the clutches of the vice, but to no avail. Eventually, he began pleading with the smith to let him go, and promised the smith to have another whole year in this world.

The smith worked very hard and acquired a good deal of wealth. When a whole year had passed, the devil came again for the smith, and, creating quite a din, insisted the smith should go with him at once. The smith said again, "Sit down on the step and wait while I finish this knife!"

The devil said he wouldn't sit down in case the same thing happened as last time. Nevertheless, he began waiting for the smith and leaned against the wall. When the smith had finished the knife, he said to the devil, "Right, off we go now!"

The devil tried but couldn't get anywhere as he was now well stuck to the wall. Then the devil, once again, began pleading with the smith to set him free and promised him another six months in this world. The smith let the devil go, and carried on working industriously, acquiring all kinds of possessions.

When six months had passed, the devil returned for the smith. The smith asked the devil to wait a little while longer, so that he could make a knife for his wife. The devil said he wouldn't wait any longer and insisted that the smith should go with him immediately. The smith then threw his pliers into the furnace and got into the devil's carriage. When the devil drove past the smith's garden, the smith said, "Let me go and pick some apples for the journey!"

The devil didn't let him go, but, instead, went

himself to shake some apples off the tree and told the smith to come and pick them up. When the devil got hold of a tree branch his hands got stuck to the tree so hard that they didn't even budge. Well, there was nothing else to do but to plead again to be set free.

The smith granted him this but only on the condition that he could now stay at home for good. The devil agreed to this, and the smith let him go. After this the smith was able to carry on his work in peace for many years.

Then he died and went to the gates of Heaven. Saint Peter was guarding the gates. He recognised the smith and said, "Go away, you evil smith! You can't come here since you've been in union with the devil!"

Then the smith went down to the entrance of Hell and tried to get in. The devil opened the door but when he noticed the smith, he exclaimed, "Away with you; so you think you'd like to come to torture me even here!"

So the smith could neither get into Heaven nor Hell, but stayed somewhere in between. This is how we get the saying, "Smiths are admitted neither into Heaven nor Hell".

The Bird Bride

nce there was a husband and a wife, who had no children. The wife said, "Go and find a bird for us; it'll do in place of a child". Well, the man went off and found a most beautiful bird. When he returned home, some girls were on their way to pick berries and asked if they could take the bird along. Well, so they went to the forest, and the bird took off her bird clothes and became a beautiful girl, so beautiful that no match could be found on land or sea. Then the other girls saw that the bird was a girl.

After they had picked the berries, they went back with the bird. The wife was very pleased that the bird had brought some berries; she was pleased to have such a bird.

The other girls were discussing how beautiful she was. The emperor's son overheard them and said, "I will take the girl for my bride!" His father protested, "Why would you take a bird for your bride; what would come of it?" The girl was given to the emperor's son, who took her home.

Well, the emperor had two sons and two daughters-in-law at home already. On Sunday he left the elder daughter-in-law at home and went to church with the others. After church they returned home and sat down to eat. The daughter-in-law wasn't very skilled at cooking. They ate. After the meal the emperor turned to his daughter-in-law. "Gather the left-over crumbs and put them in your left sleeve!"

The next morning he left his other son's wife and

went to church with the others. The daughter-in-law prepared some breakfast, but couldn't do everything to the emperor's satisfaction. He came down to breakfast and afterwards, said to his other daughter-in-law, "Gather the left-overs in your left sleeve!"

On the third morning it was the bird's turn to stay behind to prepare the breakfast. All except the bird went to church. Then the bird's bridegroom got worried. "What will come of this?" Then he rushed over to the window without anyone seeing; an extremely beautiful girl stood there. Then he ran over to an old widow.

"The girl is exceedingly beautiful and yet she is a bird. How could she be turned into a girl?"

The old widow said to him, "Enter the house through the vent. When the girl comes out into the garden, throw her bird clothes into the fire".

Well, the boy came back and slipped in through the vent and threw the clothes on the fire. The girl came in and said, "Oh, what a smell!" — as the bird clothes were burning.

Well, the boy got hold of the girl, and she changed into a rolling pin. The boy broke the pin in half. Eventually, she changed into a human being after the boy had broken everything she had turned into, even a spindle. So the girl became an exceedingly beautiful wife for the emperor's son.

The Maiden who Rose From the Sea

There was a husband and a wife, who had one son and one daughter, both exceedingly beautiful. The brother went to work for the king as a shepherd, while his sister stayed behind at home. The brother missed her greatly, often thinking of his old home. Once when the boy was out herding sheep, he drew the image of his sister on a mushroom and took it with him to the castle. The king's son happened to see it, and as the girl was so lovely and beautiful that no words could describe her, he asked to marry her there and then, and said to the brother, "Bring your sister over to the castle; I will take her for my bride and you too shall live beside me, if the daughter is as beautiful as her portrait".

The brother goes home and says to his sister, "Now, sister dear, you must come and live at the castle; the king's son wishes you for his bride". The sister, however, is not willing and says, "I shall not leave here, brother of mine, until my father's and mother's millstone shall crumble from grinding; only then will I leave my father's rooms". The brother went and broke the millstone into pieces, then put the pieces back together again, filling up the cracks here and there. When the sister went to do the grinding, the stone fell apart.

"Will you go now, sister dear?", asked the brother. "No, my brother, I shan't go yet", answered the sister, "until my father's and mother's bench will wear out from spinning". What do you know? While the sister was out, the brother chopped the bench into pieces, then put the pieces back together again. When she returned and sat down to spin, the bench splintered and fell apart.

"Will you now go, my sister?"

"No, I shall not go until my father's mortar wears out from grinding". Well, the brother went and smashed that into pieces too, then asked, "Well, now, you will go?"

"No, brother of mine, I shall not go until I wear out my mother's and father's threshold with my dress".

The brother then broke the threshold without his sister's knowledge and again asked, "Now, my sister, will you go with me?" So she left after all, taking her best clothes from the outhouse, and went off with her brother.

To get to the castle they had to travel by sea. When they were leaving the moorings, the daughter's dog, called Pilkka, trotted over and tried to get into the boat. The girl didn't have the heart to leave the dog behind, and took him with her; and so they rowed away. They had been rowing for a while, when a wicked witch, walking along the cape, called, "Take me, son of man and daughter of woman, take me along with you!"

"Shall we take her, sister?" asked the brother. "No, don't take her", answered the sister. "Evil from evil will come, evil from the seed of an evil man". They wouldn't take her and rowed on past the next cape. Again the witch came and shrieked, "Take me along on your journey!" The brother turned to his sister, "Shall I, sister, take her?"

"Better not", said the sister. "Evil from evil will

come, evil from the seed of an evil man". They didn't take her and continued rowing and came to a third cape. Again the witch is shrieking from the top of the cape, "Take me with you!" The sister doesn't want the hag to join them and says, "Don't take her!" But the brother takes her, saying, "Let us take her along, God willing". Once the witch had stepped into the boat and sat down, she took the brother's and sister's hearing, leaving them both deaf.

After travelling a while, they could see the king's castle in the distance, and the brother called to his sister from the stern of the boat, "Raise yourself from your seat, sister, adorn yourself; the king's home is in sight!" The girl, unable to hear her brother speak, asked from the bow, "What are you saying, my gentle brother?" The witch answered from the middle of the boat, "This is what your gentle brother is saying: cease your rowing, and jump into the sea!" The girl would not jump into the sea, but promptly stopped rowing, and the wicked witch took over.

After rowing a while, the brother calls for the second time, "Raise yourself from your seat, sister, adorn yourself; the king's home is in sight!"

"What are you saying, my gentle brother?" asked the sister. The witch explained from the middle of the boat, "This is what your gentle brother is saying: bare your feet, take off your clothes, and jump into the sea!" The girl then got undressed and threw her clothes to the wicked witch but did not jump into the water. They travel a while longer, when the brother says for the third time from the stern of the boat, "Raise yourself from your seat, sister, adorn yourself; the king's home is near!" The sister still could not hear him and as before asked, "What are you saying, gentle brother?"

"This is what your gentle brother is saying", the wicked witch misled her again, "Gouge your eyes out, break your arms and jump into the sea".

"Well, I suppose I must obey my one and only brother", thought the sister, and dived into the sea as she believed what her brother had said. At once the brother rushed over to reach her, but the wicked witch restrained him, saying, "Do not bother; I can look like her". She then took hold of the oars and began rowing at a great pace. The sister was left behind and drowned in the sea, and so could not be seen or heard. What was one to do? The brother dared not go to the castle without a bride and already thought of turning back, but the wicked witch was cunning; she tempted him by saying, "Take me to the castle and say I am your sister. Thus you will escape your plight and even be rewarded for your troubles".

The boy, not knowing what else to do in his distress, agreed to her plan. The wicked witch got dressed in his sister's beautiful clothes in order to look more presentable for the castle. They then continued rowing, soon reaching their destination. The king's son comes to meet them, to greet his bride, then he notices the witch and, seeing how ugly she is, asks the boy promptly, "Is this really your sister?"

"Yes, that is so".

Well, the king's son takes the wicked witch for his bride, and does not go back on his word; but as the sister's beauty was not worthy of the praise, the king's son becomes angry with the brother and says, "As the bride is not so beautiful, slaves, throw the bringer of the bride to the vipers and snakes". The slaves took him away immediately, and threw the

boy there to be eaten alive like a common criminal;
but when they came back in the morning to check up
on him, he was still in good health. They go to the
king and say, "Well, this is most strange, king's son!
Before now the vipers and snakes would eat a man in
just one night, but now the eldest snake is just resting
on the boy's lap".

"Leave things as they are; by tomorrow he will
have been eaten", answered the king's son, and told
them to take another look the next morning.

The boy's true sister, the beautiful girl, was now
living at the bottom of the sea and had been betrothed
to the sea king's son. She would otherwise have been
quite contented down there amidst so much wealth
of all kinds, but she feels pity for her brother, who,
because of the wicked witch, is being punished by
the king's son. The girl embroiders a beautiful cloth
with gold and silver, and wishes to take it to the land
king's son as a present, hoping it would help release
her brother from the company of vipers and snakes.
Well, she is allowed to take her present to the king's
son and is shackled by silver chains to prevent her
escape.

Pilkka, the girl's dog, is still alive. All day he had
been running around the castle quite lost and not
knowing who to turn to for comfort as there was no
sign of his mistress and nobody gave him any food.
When the evening came, poor Pilkka's stomach was
quite empty; he ran to the seashore where the boy's
boat was, gulped some water down and lay down in
the boat.

An old widow had a dwelling nearby, from which
a stony bridge descended into the sea, and in the
dead of night, the boy's drowned sister rose from
the sea in her silver chains—the jingle of the chains

could be heard from five versts* away—she sat on
the bridge. She looked as beautiful as before, and
her garments of silver and gold were exceedingly
handsome. The girl then noticed her dog lying on the
seashore and called to him, and putting the corner of
the cloth between his teeth, said,

> Piili**, piili, Pilkka mine,
> Open the door, undo the gate,
> Without the village folk hearing,
> Without the door creaking,
> Without the gate screeching,
> Without the black cow mooing,

"carry this cloth to the king's son's pillow, to help free
my brother from the company of vipers and snakes".
The dog went about the business at once, ran quietly
to the castle, and placed the gold cloth on the king's
son's bed while he was sleeping so that no one knew
of his visit. He then runs back the same way and
comes to his mistress on the shore. Seeing the dog,
the daughter says,

> Piili, piili, Pilkka mine,
> Come and tell me
> Where my brother is!

Pilkka answered,

> Over there is your brother
> Amongst the vipers and snakes.

The daughter asked again,

---

* An old Finnish measure of length (*Suomen virsta*), approx.
1069 m (1169 yd); the Swedish verst is approx. 2672 m (2935 yd)
and the Russian 1067 m.

** This is a nonsense word, present only for the alliteration.

What news have you
From my bridegroom's home?

Pilkka answered,

I'll tell you this:
The wicked witch is in your place
Stretching herself beside the groom.

The daughter asked,

What did they eat at the wedding,
At the wedding of the witch,
At the feast of the wicked one,
At the orgy of the ogress,
At the banquet of the long-tailed one?

Pilkka answered,

The bones from the meat,
The heads from the fish,
All the peelings from the turnips,
The burnt crusts of bread.

"Come to me again for two more nights and lie on the shore; I will need you", said the daughter and jumped from the bridge back into the sea and returned to the home of the sea king as she had promised when she left.

When the morning comes, the king's son got up and, to his surprise, finds a cloth on his pillow and says, "I wonder where this delicately embroidered scarf has come from?" The wicked witch, lying through her teeth, said to her husband, "Well, I like that—all you can do is just lie there and doze, while I embroider a gold cloth in the night for you". However, the king's son did not believe her, and thought to himself, "This is not your needlework; something like this cannot be accomplished in one night". All the castle folk were questioned about any possible night visitors but to no avail and, as the owner of the cloth could not be found, the matter was put to rest.

The king's son then remembered the one amidst the snakes and ordered his slaves to go and clear the bones away, as the boy will now have been eaten. Well, the slaves went to check on the boy but soon returned, saying, "He has not been eaten, the eldest snake just keeps resting on the boy's lap, in his arms". The king's son, thinking this to be most odd, goes over to the old widow. "My dear old widow, when I threw a man amidst the vipers and snakes, how is it that he, for two nights, has not yet been eaten, when it used to take only one night to be eaten?"

"Why did you throw him there?" asked the old widow. The king's son replied, "When I hired a handsome boy for my shepherd, he told me he had a sister who was still more beautiful, and I asked her to be my bride. The brother brought his sister over to the castle, but when I saw her she was so ugly, that I threw the liar amongst the vipers and snakes. However, I did not go back on my word and took his sister for my bride".

"That is not his sister", said the old widow. "His true sister is at the bottom of the sea, from where she brought a cloth and left it on your pillow, so that you might set her brother free. The wicked witch is your bride!"

With this knowledge, the king's son leaves the old widow and returns home. He spends a whole day deep in thought until night falls. The daughter is again preparing to rise from the sea, and take a gift to the king's son as she did before; she is sewing him a shirt with threads of gold and silver. Again she is shackled with silver chains and allowed to rise from the seabed.

In the dead of the night she arrives—you can hear the tinkle of her chains five versts away—she rises and sits on the end of the bridge by the old widow's dwelling, wearing bright and exceedingly beautiful garments of silver and gold. She then speaks to her dog.

> Piili, piili, Pilkka mine,
> Open the door, undo the gate,
> Without the village folk hearing,
> Without the door creaking,
> Without the gate screeching,
> Without the black cow mooing,
> Carry this shirt to the king's son's pillow.

Pilkka took the shirt between his teeth, and carried it to the king's son's pillow as he had been told to do. The next morning when the king's son awakens and sees the golden shirt on his pillow, he says, "Who has placed this shirt on my pillow?"

"O my gracious king's son!" said the witch, "I lie here, but my hands are awake and busy; this is what I sew, this is what I knit, while you just lie there and get all puffed up".

Just then the slaves arrived and said, "O merciful king's son! The one amidst the vipers and snakes will not die; the eldest snake is still resting on his lap".

"Well, you had better remove him, since the snakes will not eat him", replied the king and told his slaves to leave. The king's son put on the shirt he had found on his pillow and went over to visit the old widow, thinking, "This needlework is not my woman's work, she cannot sew like this". When he arrives at the old widow's cottage he says to her, "My dear old widow, tell me what is going on; the first night a golden cloth is placed on my pillow, and the second night a golden shirt is placed on my pillow?"

"That is strange indeed, my boy", answered the old widow; "In the night a young maiden rises from the sea and stops at the steps to my dwelling; she is adorned in gold and silver, and is so beautiful, so beautiful that no song or verse can describe her, and she always brings a gift for you. That is who your true bride is, and the one whom you keep as your wife is the wicked witch".

The king's son then had a desire to see the one who had brought him such gifts, and said to the old woman, "How could I meet this beautiful maiden, should she rise from the sea again?"

"She will bring you one more gift", said the old woman, "but after that she will become the wife of the sea king's son. Call at the blacksmith's workshop and have him forge you a scythe and long iron chains and come here tonight to wait and watch. When you see the daughter rise up from the sea get hold of her at once with your chains and with the scythe cut through the manacles by which she is shackled and don't let her go, whatever she may turn into, but destroy every transformation with your weapons; eventually she will turn into a human". The king's son went to the blacksmith immediately, had the scythe and and the chains forged and returned later that night to watch by the bridge.

He stands there waiting for a while, but there is no

51

sign of her coming. At last, in the dead of night, a jingling sound is heard from the distance, and a maiden, so lovely and beautiful that no words could describe her, begins to rise from the sea. She sits on the steps by the bridge and turns to her dog, saying, "Piili, piili, Pilkka of mine, take these trousers to the king's son's bed!" Just then the king's son emerged from his hiding place and tried to catch the maiden as the old woman had advised.

The maiden tried to throw herself back into the sea, but the king's son was prepared—he at once threw the chains around her to stop her escaping. He then grabbed his scythe and cut through the maiden's rattling chains, which slipped back into the sea. The maiden still tried to escape from him, she turned into an earthworm, then a flying insect, then a lizard, then a snake, then a spindle, then a rolling pin and many other things; but the king's son destroyed them all, and would not give up until she had once more become human and regained her lovely form.

"What do you, king's son, want from me, as the witch is sure to eat me anyway?" said the maiden. "Do not worry", said the king's son, "she will not stay in my castle for much longer; you will be reunited with your only brother who has already been freed". He took the daughter to the old woman where they spent the night. In the morning he left the daughter in the care of the old woman, and went home to his castle. There his old bride asks him, "Where have you been walking, my bridegroom; you do not seem to care much for your home?"

"Worry not, I shall never disregard you for even a week", said the king's son; but he turned to his slaves and said, "Heat up the iron stove in the sauna. Dig a grave three fathoms deep under the threshold, fill it with tar and set fire to it, then place a brown cloth over the grave, then stretch some blue cloth from the threshold of the sauna to the door of the castle; upon it you will lead my bride to the sauna".

The slaves did everything to the letter and were leading the witch to the sauna just as they had done with this king's son's bride before; one carried her skirts, another one guided her by the hand. When they reached the sauna door, the witch said, "I need not be led any longer; I shall jump onto the threshold from here and then on to the benches. But the slaves coaxed her by saying, "Do step down, the king's son's only bride, along the smooth surface, along the brown bridge".

The witch then stepped onto the cloth, and immediately it was pulled from under her feet and she plunged into the grave, three fathoms deep, where she was left. While burning, she pulled hair from her head and yelled, "Let my hair become the insects of the air, the worms of the earth, the maggots of Death to plague mankind forever!"

Now that he was rid of the witch, the king's son went to the old widow and took the beautiful maiden, who had risen from the sea, for his bride and they celebrated their wedding at the castle. The king's son then took the brother of his bride for his trusted man and gave him half his wealth for having such a beautiful sister. And that is all.

The Death of the Wicked Witch

nce upon a time there was a king's son who had a beautiful bride. This caused the wicked witch great envy. One day the young king (*sic*) went out rowing with his bride. The witch came to the end of the cape and called out, "Won't you take me along in your boat!" The king wouldn't take her. So the witch rushed over to another cape and called out again, "Do take me with you, please!" The king didn't want to do that, but his bride said, "Oh, let's take her along; we're not going to be rid of her otherwise!"

The witch was taken into the boat. As soon as she was in the boat, the witch put a spell on the bride so that she couldn't hear the king speak, although she could hear the witch perfectly well.

The king was saying affectionate things to his bride, but she couldn't hear him. The bride asked the witch, "What is the king saying?"

"The king says you should hang yourself!"

The bride thought that this request was too severe and couldn't fulfil it. Again the king spoke kind words, and his bride asked, "What is the king saying?" The wicked woman answered, "The king wants you to jump in the lake!"

Again the bride thought this was really terrible, but because he had always been so kind to her, she did as he had asked and jumped into the lake. The king tried to get hold of his bride, but in vain.

Now the witch enchanted the king so that he began caressing the witch and, eventually, took the witch for his wife.

The king's previous bride was now living at the bottom of the lake, and the king's faithful dog carried letters from there to him. The king wrote to his bride asking her how to get rid of the wicked witch. The bride wrote, "Prepare the sauna and light a furnace under the doorway. Strech out a fine piece of cloth over the furnace to cover it. When the witch will step on it, she will fall into the flames and burn. Only then will I be free to leave this place".

The king followed her advice and prepared the sauna alongwith the furnace underneath. He then invited the witch to go and bathe in the sauna. When she stepped on the cloth, she fell straight into the furnace and was burnt. This is how the wicked witch died.

The king's bride came to live with the king in his castle, and they are still living there happily.

The Devoted Orphans

n a hamlet there was a cottage in which a brother and a sister lived alone, as their mother and father had died. They loved each other dearly. The brother worked to support them both. One day the king's son happened to be passing by—he was looking for a workman. He stopped at the cottage and asked the boy to go with him. The boy didn't really want to go, but had no choice. When they arrived at the king's castle, the boy was set to work raking muck. He missed his sister dreadfully and often cried from his longing for her.

Once when he was so overcome with longing for his sister, he drew her portrait on the wall. When the king's son saw it, he asked whose work the drawing was. The boy said it was a portrait of his sister. The king's son asked if his sister really was that beautiful. The boy replied, "I am unable to draw her true beauty". The king's son said, "If she is that beautiful, she can be my wife". The boy then went to ask his sister to come to the castle. She didn't want to leave her home, but knew that she must.

While crossing the lake, they came to a cape, where they saw a wicked witch with her daughter. The witch called, "Take us into your boat!" They refused. When they came to a second cape, the witch again called, "Take us into your boat!" This time they took the witch and her daughter into the boat. When the evil woman stepped into the boat, she put plugs into the beautiful girl's ears, so that she could hear nothing but the witch. Then the brother said to his sister, "Wash your eyes, we're approaching the king's manor".

The witch then said to the girl, "Can't you hear what your brother is saying: 'Jump into the lake, you devil!'" After a little while the brother said again, "Wash your eyes, sister dear, we're near the king's manor". His sister said, "My brother's lips are moving, but I can't hear what he is saying".

"Listen, your brother is telling you to jump into the lake, you devil!" said the wicked witch. After a while the brother again told his sister to wash her eyes, as they were nearing the king's manor. "My brother's lips are moving, but I can't hear what he is saying", said the sister. And again the wicked witch said to the girl, "Listen, you devil, your brother is telling you to jump into the lake!" The girl jumped into the lake.

When they arrived at the shore, the king's son came to meet them. When he saw the girl in the boat the king's son was very disappointed, because she looked so nasty. He had to take her, as he had already promised. However, he locked the boy down in the dungeon, then took the girl and her mother into the castle.

When the sister had jumped into the lake she was betrothed to the water king's son. She was clothed in fine garments and was quite contented. Once she said, "Let me go and visit my brother; he lives up there in the clouds". She was granted permission to visit her brother. The king fastened gold chains to her hands and feet, and said, "When I tug your chains, you must return". When the girl rose up to the ground, the whole shore brightened up. When she walked past the king's manor, even the walls became bright, and the gold chains jingled and

jangled as she walked. The girl opened the doors
quietly, so that the guard wouldn't notice. She then
came to her brother, and they put their arms round
each other and wept. The girl said to her brother,
"When they give a tug on the chains, I must leave".
The night passed, and she felt a tug on the chains and
left. The following night the girl came to her brother
and again she wept with her brother. When she felt
the tug, she had to leave. The guard happened to see
her and told the king's son what had happened. The
next time the girl was preparing to go to her brother,
the king said, "You may go once more; after that we
shall arrange your wedding".

Now that the king's son knew about the beautiful
girl, he went to the shore with his men who were
armed with axes and saws. When the girl rose from
the water, the whole shore brightened up because of
her beauty. When she stepped onto the shore, the men
cut her chains which fell down into the hands of the
water king. When the girl met her brother, she said
to him, "This is the last time that I may visit you".
But when the day broke, she didn't feel the tug. The
king's son then came to the prison and saw the girl.
"Now I know that this is your real sister", he said to
the boy.

They were taken to the castle, but weren't shown
to the wicked witch. The boy tried to think of a way
how he could get rid of the witch. She was a great
sauna-lover and had the sauna heated every night.
The boy said to the workmen, "Heat up the sauna
and dig a deep pit in the floor of the sauna, fill it
with tar and fire and then cover it with a carpet".
When the wicked witch and her daughter came to
bathe, the wicked witch said to her daughter, "I'll
take a long jump from the threshold". But the girl

said, "We have to step daintily on tiptoes". As they did so, they drowned in the burning tar. And that's all.

~ ~ ~

The Castle of Snakes

The king's son had courted the daughter of an old witch, but had not married her. This had angered the witch so much that she turned the entire kingdom into a sandy heath and all its inhabitants into snakes. Only the king's castle was left standing in the midst of the sands. The enchantment would only end if a girl fell in love with the king's son, who was now in the form of a snake.

A merchant was setting off on a long journey with his servant and when bidding farewell, his daughter said, "Father, bring me a beautiful flower". The merchant promised to do so and began his journey. One day on their way back home, they came to the vast, sandy heath. They kept driving on until the horses grew tired. It was so dark that one couldn't see any light or a road. At long last they could see lights shining from many windows in one direction and headed towards the light, even though the horses were very tired. The light shone down from a big, beautiful castle.

They drove into the courtyard; there was nobody about, but everything looked in good order, as if some people had only just left it. As it was dark, they had to put up for the night. The servant led the horses into the stable while the master went indoors and walked through every room. But there was no one to be seen, although each room had a fire burning.

They then went together into a somewhat poorer room and sat down on the couch; they felt very tired and soon fell asleep. When the servant woke up he saw a table laid with coffee and buns in front of them. He woke his master, and together they wondered where it all had come from, but as they were hungry, what else was there to do, but to eat and drink? After drinking some coffee they went back to sleep. While they were sleeping the coffee was cleared away and replaced with some food. Again they were thoroughly bemused, but the merchant was a brave man, as merchants usually are, and told his servant to eat as he did himself, saying that he would leave some money for the night's lodging should they not see anyone before leaving.

After their meal the servant went to check the horses, who also had food in front of them although he himself had not given them any. In another room two beds had been made, and so the men, being still sleepy, went to bed.

When they woke up in the morning, there was already coffee and coffee-bread by the bed, together with water and towels for washing. They also had some gruel, and then the servant began harnessing the horses. Meanwhile the master visited each room in the castle but did not meet a living soul. In one room he saw a beautiful flower and remembered that his daughter had asked him to bring back a beautiful flower. He thought, "What good was a beautiful flower in an empty room?" and took it with him. Just as he was about to get into his carriage, a large snake appeared from under the building and said, "Since you took the flower, you'll have to stay in the castle forever, or promise to give me your daughter".

The merchant was greatly frightened when the snake spoke to him of such things but as one's own life is more precious than someone else's, he promised to give his daughter away. The snake sent a carriage with them which was to bring the girl to the castle, and the merchant left for home feeling sad.

As soon as he got home, his daughter came to meet him in the yard and asked, "Father, have you brought me a beautiful flower?" Well, the merchant told her everything that had happened in the castle. The girl thought that she would go quite willingly. So she went and sat in the carriage which left for the castle, where she settled.

There was always food, although the girl had no idea where it was coming from as she always grew drowsy when the food was brought in or taken away. There was beautiful furniture in every room, and everything was fine and grand. Every time she sat down on the couch or somewhere else, the snake came over and licked her ankles, shins and thighs. At first the girl thought it wrong, but gradually she got used to it and eventually began to desire it. Once the snake said to her, "Do you miss your parents?"

"I do, a great deal!" said the girl.

"Over there, there is a chamber with a special mirror; when one looks into it, one sees the image of that which one holds dearest. But one mustn't cry or the image will disappear," advised the snake. The girl went over and looked into the mirror. There were her parents, quite lifelike. Every time she missed them she would go and look in the mirror. But once she started to cry and couldn't see anything anymore. When she sat down on the couch, the snake asked, "Did you see anything now?"

"No," said the girl.

"You shouldn't have cried," said the snake.

As the girl could no longer see her parents, her longing grew. Once the snake said to her, "Would you like to go and see your home?"

"I would indeed," said the girl.

"Tomorrow you may go," said the snake. But there was a condition that after a few days' stay she should leave at midnight, right on the last stroke of twelve.

The girl's visit caused much joy at home. But she failed to get into the carriage in time for twelve o'clock. When she finally got to the castle, there was no castle there at all, only the garden; the castle had disappeared under the ground or wherever. The girl walked into the garden and she felt such longing that she burst into tears. Then she spotted a line on the path which she followed to the well. Just then the girl became so overwhelmed with longing that she jumped into the well. The snake had gone there, too, and when the girl saw it she embraced it. At that very moment the well turned into the castle, and the sandy heath into the kingdom, and all the snakes into inhabitants, and the large snake into the king's son. Great joy filled the castle, then there was a wonderful wedding celebration, and the rest you understand yourself.

Antti Puuhaara

wo men, well versed in wisdom, happened to come by a cottage where they asked to rest for the night. However, in the main room there was already a guest—a rich merchant of fox skins, who had arrived earlier and was now having a rest. As the farmer's wife was ailing, the farmer was unable to offer better lodgings for his new guests than those of the stable loft, and hoped that this would do. The men were satisfied with this and, feeling tired after their journey, went to their quarters, which they found excellent for resting as it happened to be a lovely summer's evening.

While they were lying there, in the middle of the night, they could hear a sorry wailing from the cottage as the farmer's wife was in labour, and this had awoken the seers. Said one man to the other, "Help this wife in her suffering; it is so sad to listen to her wailing".

"It is not the time to help yet", answered the elder seer, turning over on his side. "But when there's the need, there's always the time", asserted the other, resenting his companion's talk. "Well, actually, I have already helped her as far as I could", was the elder seer's comment; and as he was saying this the farmer's wife already had a small boy in her arms. Then the other man again turns to his friend, "Well, what kind of man will the child grow into, I wonder?" "I should think he will inherit the riches of the merchant, who is spending the night in the cottage", answered the head seer, and went back to sleep.

What do you know; the merchant, unable to find peace for the child's crying, went for a walk in the garden. He happened to overhear the seers' conversation from the stable, which set him thinking all night so much so that he was unable to catch any sleep. Having pondered the matter, the merchant finally decided to drown the new-born child by whatever means, in order to prevent the seers' prediction from coming true. In the morning, with this plan in mind, he had a chat with the cottagers, lamenting that such a poor man had so many children, and then treacherously asked if he could adopt their newborn son, saying that he, who was richer would raise the boy to be a man. Well, the parents, who already had many children to support, agreed to the idea; they wished a better future for their child with the rich man, better than he would have in their poor home. And so they gave their youngest son, who had been born in the night, to the merchant. The merchant was very happy at their decision and tried many ways to satisfy the mother with all kinds of things and even gave her money for the upkeep of her other children.

He took his leave from the cottage, taking the little adopted son and feeling pleased with himself, as he believed he had made a good deal. However, his thoughts towards the child were very black. As the journey took him through a dark forest, the merchant soon stopped by the wayside and hung his adopted son from a tree branch, thinking that his heir was sure to die in the forest and thus the prediction would not come true.

But what happened? The merchant had barely restarted his journey when a hunter happened to be walking the same way through the dark forest and heard the child crying. He heads towards the sound and, to his surprise, sees a small male child there on a tree branch suffering miserably. No sooner had the hunter seen this than he climbed the tree, picked up the child, covered him up and took him home. There he acquired a wet nurse for the child and brought him up as if he were his own. Thus the boy grew up strong and handsome, and the adopted father called him Antti; but the village urchins, upon hearing the true origins of the boy, gave him the nickname Puuhaara*, and soon everyone was calling him by that name.

Many years went by, perhaps a decade or so, and Antti had grown up to be a man. One day the same old fox skin merchant happened to be walking his old route and dropped by the hunter's home for the night, as he had no wish to stay with the cottager, from whom he had once, long ago, taken the child. During his stay the merchant learned that the young man of the house was called Antti Puuhaara, which sounded most strange to him. Wondering at this he eventually asked his host how had the boy been given such an unusual name. The master of the house told him how he had found the boy as a baby suspended from a tree branch and had taken him as his adopted son, as he had no children of his own, and so explained that this is how the boy had acquired his nickname. The merchant was greatly startled at this talk and soon guessed what had happened, but decided to keep his thoughts to himself. He only said, "Well, that is a strange story

*Puuhaara: the fork of a tree, a branch.

indeed, never heard anything like it!" He never said anything else and pretended to have forgotten the whole thing and went to bed. However, he kept pondering over a way to get rid of the boy so that the seers' prediction would not come true, as it still terrified him.

The night passed and, when morning came, the merchant started talking to his host: "I have some important business at home, but cannot really go myself; I was wondering that perhaps your adopted son might take a letter there for me?"

"Well, I don't see why not", answered the hunter, and sent Antti on the rich man's errand, hoping that he would get a good reward for his efforts. But the merchant only had evil intentions. In his letter he had given instructions to capture the messenger and hang him from the birch that grew by the side of his manor. Antti had no idea of this and, therefore, could not suspect deception and so went on his errand as his father had ordered.

After walking for a day or so he came to the foot of a mountain where, in the shade of some trees, it was pleasant to rest on the moss. He sat down feeling tired and soon dropped off to sleep without knowing, still holding the merchant's letter in his hand. Two students happened to be passing by and saw the letter in the hands of the sleeper and, with mischief in mind, began to read the letter. After seeing what had been written and realising the treachery of the writer, they in turn decided to deceive the merchant. On their travels they had visited the merchant's house many a time and were very familiar with the running of the house, and how things were there. The other student sat down on a stone and, copying the merchant's handwriting, changed the meaning of the message. "When the bringer of this letter arrives", it now read, "he should be given to my daughter in marriage without fail, as I have promised him so myself, whereas Musti, my dog who is already long in the tooth, should have a cord tied round his neck and be hanged from the birch that grows in the garden. These orders of mine should be carried out without delay before my return, or else you will not be pleased with your payment". Having finished writing, the students placed it back in the hands of the sleeping lad and left without waking him, so the lad knew nothing of what had taken place.

Having slept for a while, Antti Puuhaara woke up and continued his journey, stepping vigorously until he arrived at the house where he gave the letter to the house dwellers to read. The mistress of the house takes the letter and reads it aloud for everyone to hear. Well, well, they thought this a strange request indeed, but as they recognised the master's handwriting, it was no good contemplating the matter much further. The daughter of the house was given to Antti Puuhaara in marriage, and the old Musti was hanged from the big birch that grew by the house just as it was stated in the letter.

A few weeks passed, and the merchant returned home. Already from a distance he could see something black hanging from the birch that grew next to the house. Delighted by the fact that it must be Antti Puuhaara hanging up there in the distance, the merchant lashed his horse with a whip, as he could hardly wait to reach his house, saying to himself, "Aha! My dear Antti, how long have you been swinging there? You will not inherit from me now, will you?" Then, as he arrived at the house, how his mood suddenly changed when he saw his faithful Musti hanging dead from the birch, whereas Antti Puuhaara, alive and well, was coming to greet him along with the rest of the household! He had his wits about him, though, and managed to hide his anger. Instead, he turned to his wife who now told him everything, and that his letter had been forged, which was the reason why Antti Puuhaara was now his son-in-law.

He then went over to Antti and, greeting him, said, "Well, now that you are my son-in-law and will probably one day inherit all my wealth, I think it only fair that you should work for it and prove to me that you deserve it. All my life I have been contemplating what kind of occupation would make Man happiest—I myself finally became a merchant; but this work no longer satisfies me and I would like to find out what kind of work would suit me best. Now I want you to go and seek this information. Go to Pohjola* and ask Louhi** what makes Man happy. When you have found the answer, you may return home".

Antti, unaware of the deception, agreed to the demands of his father-in-law. It never occurred to the boy that the intention might have been for him never to return from his journey and so, with a stick in his hand, he set off to discover the information his father-in-law had asked for. After walking a good while, he comes across Hiisi's*** rock—a monster of

---

Pohjola: a cold, dark region in the North associated with death, evil and knowledge.

**Louhi*: the ruler of Pohjola; the Witch of the North.

***Hiisi*: a mighty giant or demon; the protector of nature.

a mountain on top of which a terribly tall and fiercelooking man is standing and supporting a cluster of clouds on his head, and whose cap holds the nest for eight gusts of wind. He notices Antti and asks gently, "Where are you travelling to, my son?"

"I am on my way to Pohjola to ask Louhi how Man can find happiness", Antti replied.

"While you are there, dear boy, find out something for me", said the giant. "I have an orchard which used to produce plenty of beautiful fruit, but now everything just turns to mould; ask how I could improve my orchard, I shall give you my best stallion for your journey".

"I will find out for you", answered Antti, and took the Hiisi stallion from the giant and set off.

After riding for a while, Antti heard a terrific rumble, and the earth began to shake. Bewildered at the noise, he rushed forth and, after riding some distance, he came to a large stone castle where incredible things appeared to him. At the castle gate there stands an enormously broad and tall man holding a huge key in his hand. At times he would blow on the key and then try to open the door, but as he cannot get the key into the lock he pounds on the door so hard that the whole neighbourhood echoes noisily and the foundations of the castle tremble. Finding himself in a din such as this was, poor Antti was thoroughly frightened, so much so that he was shaking in his trousers. But once he got used to the rumble he regained his composure and bravely approached the man who was standing on the steps and wished him good day. The giant, although angrily scratching the back of his ear, on hearing the greeting turned towards Antti and asked, "Where are you going, my son?"

"I am on my way to Pohjola", said Antti, "to ask Louhi how Man finds happiness".

"Well, since you are going there, my fellow", said the giant, "you could find out where the real keys to my castle are, as I cannot get the door open. If you bring me this information, I will give you my best treasure as payment".

"I shall do that", answered Antti and, bidding the giant goodbye, continued his journey. As he was travelling on the Hiisi stallion he was advancing at a great pace and after a while saw another Hiisi castle atop another mountain before him. On the mountain there grew a large, tall pine and on the treetop sat a giant holding an terrifically long spear in his hand. A large bonfire was burning on the ground and the tree-sitter was roasting an entire elk on his spear over the fire. No sooner had the giant spotted Antti that he turned to him, saying, "Come, come! Hurry up my boy, get a few pieces of roast into your stomach!" Antti, whose stomach was rumbling from hunger, could not have guessed there would be a roast ready and waiting when he rode up the mountain on the splendid stallion. Having had his fill of elk meat he wished to continue his journey, but the tree-sitter was delaying him with his chatter, asking, "Why are you in such a hurry, where are you heading to from here?"

"I am on my way to Pohjola", answered Antti, "to learn from Louhi what makes Man the happiest".

"Well, while you are there, ask her why do I have to sit in a tree all my life? At times I manage to spear an elk or some other creature, but when the forest fails to provide, I am often at the point of dying from hunger".

"I shall find out the answer for you", answered

Antti, and thanking the giant for the food, jumped on his stallion and rode off.

After riding a good distance, however long that may have been, Antti comes to a wide river. There is a small boat by the bank, and in that boat sits a hook-chinned old hag with a paddle under her arm. Well, Antti, seeing no other way of getting across the river, turned to the one sitting in the boat and asked, "Could a traveller get across the river in your boat?"

"Indeed, he can", answered the old woman. "One should help a fellow, after all, but where will you leave your horse?"

"I shall leave him here on the bank to await my return; it seems there is some lush grass growing here", said Antti, and after tying up his stallion he went into the boat. During the crossing the old woman starts talking and asks Antti, "From where and on what business has the visitor come to these faraway lands?"

"From such and such", said Antti. "I am on my way to Pohjola to ask Louhi, how Man can find happiness; is there still far to go, I wonder?"

"Louhi's house is not far from here", answered the old woman. "You will soon reach your destination; once on dry land, keep heading straight on and you will soon see Pohjola; but when you arrive there, ask for me, dear stranger, why do I have to keep endlessly taking travellers across the river? Forty years I have been doing this ferrying and now that I am in my old age I would like to leave this job".

"I will find out for you", answered Antti, and stepping off the boat he thanked the old woman and continued his journey on foot.

He did not have to walk far before he reached habitation and soon caught a glimpse of a house.

Antti, guessing from the old woman's description that it had to be Louhi's home, walked down the hill to the yard and from the yard into the farmhouse kitchen. The mistress of the house was not about, only the daughter, by herself, kneading dough at the kitchen table. Antti walked in wishing the daughter good day, sat down on the bench, and was soon asking the whereabouts of the mistress. "My mother is not at home", answered the girl, "but if you have the time to wait until the evening, she will return for the night". Hearing this, Antti Puuhaara settled down to wait until the evening.

To pass the time, he discussed this and that with the daughter, who in turn wanted to know where the stranger had come from and what business had brought him to wander so far. "I am from such and such place", replied Antti. "I have all sorts of things to ask your mother". He mentioned the things he needed to find answers to. "Oh, dear!" said the girl after Antti had finished. "These are no small things you need answers to. I wonder if mother will be able to provide them; but listen, I may be able to find out for you. When my mother returns at nightfall you had better hide behind the oven, so that she would not see you. By listening carefully to what we say, you will find out the information you are looking for, and then you may leave secretly during the night". The boy was strong and handsome, you see, and the girl took pity on him.

Antti Puuhaara spent the whole day with the daughter in the farmhouse kitchen; they spent hours talking but in the evening he hid behind the oven, as he had been advised to, in wait for the mistress of the house. He remains in his hiding place until nightfall, when Louhi returns and asks her daughter if there had been any visitors while she was out. "There was a man who had called in to ask all kinds of things", answered the girl, "but as you were not at home, he went off to find the information elsewhere".

"Well, well", said Louhi, "what could that be that others might know better than me? Did he say, that man, what he wanted to know?"

"Ah, he did that", replied the daughter. "His first question was that how can Man find happiness".

"Now, there is a cunning enquirer, to ask things like that", said Louhi. "I would have hardly given him the answer at all, and a sheer waste of time it would be to ask anybody else. What he was asking, nobody else in the whole world knows the answer to, and I should not willingly part with the information myself, but as it has come up now, I shall just say this: Man is happiest when digging earth; trees have to be pulled by the roots from the ground, rocks shifted into piles and the ground cleared for a field instead". After her mother's answer the daughter continued, "His second question was: what was wrong with the orchard of one giant, as now it is growing mould where, previously, beautiful fruit would grow in abundance?".

"That is an easy one to answer, too", said Louhi. "A worm is growing in that giant's garden which dries the fruit with its breath, if the worm was killed between two stones, the orchard would return to its previous glory, producing plenty of fruit. Was there anything else he wanted to know?"

"He had many questions", answered the daughter. "Apparently there was a giant who could not get into his castle, so the traveller asked where the real keys could be found; despite many attempts, the door would not open".

"Dear me, what a thing to ask!" said Louhi. "Why, the keys are under the steps; all he needs to do is to lift the top flight of the steps, and there he would find the keys. Was there anything else he asked?"

"There was", said the daughter. "It seems there is a giant who has spent all his life sitting up a tree, and he was asking how does a tree-sitter get down onto the ground again?".

"Well, that would not need any drastic measures, either", said Louhi. "Nothing more than to understand how to push an alder staff into the roots of that tree. The top of the tree would then tumble down in a mass of gold to the ground, and the man would be able to move about wherever he liked. I do not suppose he asked anything else, did he?"

"One more thing", said the daughter. "How could the old woman be relieved from the ferrying duties, she who takes travellers across the river".

"Woe to that old crone, she is quite soft in the head!" said Louhi. "When the next traveller arrives, she should take him across the river and then jump ahead onto the bank and with her left heel push the boat back, saying, 'I will be off now, you stay behind in the boat!' Thus she would free herself from the ferryman's job, and the other person would have to take her place. Have we come to the end of the questions yet?"

"We have, the traveller did not ask anything else".

Antti Puuhaara, hiding behind the oven, listened to them talk and memorised Louhi's replies well, then waited for an opportunity to leave the house. It was not long before he could hear loud snoring coming from the farmhouse kitchen where he guessed Louhi was sleeping; quietly he lowered himself from his hiding place down to the floor, then tiptoed to the door. From there he quickly slipped into the yard and headed for home, walking quickly; he soon found himself at the river bank where the old woman was sitting just as before. She spotted Antti and called to him from the boat, "Did you, dear stranger, manage to find out about my business?"

"I did, indeed", said Antti Puuhaara, "but take me across the river first, then I will tell you". The old woman agreed and took Antti to the opposite bank, where she again enquired how she might be freed from being the ferryman. "Do not fret", he answered. "When the next person comes and asks you to take him across the river, do as you have always done, but once you have reached the bank, do not let him out of the boat. Instead, jump out yourself first and push the boat back into the river with your left heel, saying, 'I will be off now, you stay here!' Thus you will be freed from your duty, and the other person will stay in your place".

The old woman was thoroughly delighted, thanked Antti many times for the advice and sat down in her boat to wait for the next traveller who would be the one to inherit her job. Antti took his stallion which he had left at the river bank and rode off as fast as he could. On his way he came to the mountain where he had been eating the elk meat earlier. There the giant was still sitting at the top of the pine as before and called to Antti from a distance, "Hello, my son; did you get the answers for me?"

"I did, indeed", answered Antti, "but wait a little". He went and broke off an alder branch and with it struck at the roots of the pine; the treetop tumbled down to the ground in a mass of gold, and so did the giant. When he got to his feet, he began jumping, rocking merrily, and said to Antti, "Now that you have done this merciful deed for me and let me come down from the tree, how should I reward you?"

"I am not expecting any reward", said Antti, "but if you wish to give me a present, give me a few branches of this pine top that has just fallen to the ground".

"Yes, you may have them", said the giant, and broke off a whole bunch of gold branches from the fallen treetop for Antti's present. "Thank you for your gift", said Antti. "I can use these to hurry my stallion along". He climbed onto his stallion and rode off. He soon came to another castle, where he saw the giant with the key standing by the steps. Antti advised him of the whereabouts of the keys to the castle and received the giant's best treasure for his reward as promised. He rode off with all this treasure and came to the third castle, the Hiisi castle, whose guardian had given the stallion to Antti. When he informed the giant how his orchard would improve from having the worm killed, the worm whose breath had dried up the fruit, Antti was rewarded with the stallion, and they rode off home.

The father-in-law is greatly surprised to see Antti Puuhaara return home, as he had wished and thought him dead long ago, and asks him in annoyance, "Have you got the answer to the question already, seeing that you are back so soon?"

"Indeed I have!" replied Antti. "My task is complete".

"Well, what makes Man the happiest?" asked the merchant.

"Man is happiest when he is digging earth",

answered Antti. "Trees must be pulled from the ground by their roots, rocks shifted into piles and the ground cleared for a field, this is what Louhi advised". Well, it was greatly paining the merchant's heart to see that he still could not get rid of his son-in-law, but when he found out about the riches that Antti had accumulated on his travels, he became really depressed. Feeling much envy towards his son-in-law, the merchant found it impossible to cope at home, and leaving his entire house for Antti Puuhaara to look after, set off for the same journey as Antti, hoping he would come to the same fortune.

After travelling a while the merchant came to the riverbank, as Antti had done, and tried to cross the river bank as Antti had done. There the same old woman is sitting in her boat as before and waiting for a traveller, whom she could pass her job onto. She very eagerly takes the merchant into her boat, but when approaching the other side she jumped onto the river bank and with her left heel pushed the boat back into the river, saying, "I will be off now, you stay here!" This is how the merchant of fox skins became the ferryman of the river just as Louhi had said, and that is where he will stay as nobody has any more business with Louhi, now that Antti Puuhaara had gained his knowledge from her, and every Finn knows how to find happiness.

Thus Antti Puuhaara remained master in his father-in-law's house and lived happily with his wife, and eventually inherited the rich merchant's wealth just as had been predicted.

The Old Man's Daughter and the Old Woman's Daughters

A man had just one daughter until he took a second wife. His new wife had two daughters who would wash themselves every day in the hope that the king would marry one of them. They hated their stepsister and would only give her porridge to eat. She was very, very lovely, and much more beautiful than her step-mother's daughters.

Once the old woman was baking and the stepdaughter asked, "Give me a small cake, mother dear, so that for once I may know what it tastes like!" The old woman baked a small cake but, while cooking, the cake began to swell greatly. The old woman got very angry and threw the cake into the yard, and so the daughter chased after it, but the cake began rolling down the road so fast that she couldn't catch it. The daughter met an old man who said, "Would you pat my head, my girl?"

"I haven't the time", said the girl. "I must run after my cake!"

"Oh, it'll stop to wait for you", said the old man.

The girl patted the man's head and when she stopped, the cake began to roll once again, and so the girl chased after it.

The cake rolled into a crofter's cottage before the girl was able to catch it. There an old woman said, "Stay with me and do the housework. I'll reward you for your work". The girl stayed, and the old woman told her to begin by feeding the cows. The girl fed the cows and gently stroking them praised their plump bodies. When the girl had finished the housework, the old woman told her to go to the sauna to bathe the lizards and was told to wash them really well. The girl went and bathed them and, having washed them really well, put them to bed. Then the old woman told her to clean the frogs. The girl went off and washed the frogs and cleaned their den very well. Then the girl went to the old woman who said, "Sit yourself down here, while I pop out".

The old woman went to her cows and asked, "Did you have a good maid?"

"Yes, she was very good indeed", replied the cows. "We've never had anybody so good. She stroked and petted us well, gave us a drink and made us feel good".

The old woman then went into the sauna and asked the lizards, "Did you have a good maid?"

"Yes, she was so good", said the lizards, "that we've never before had anyone so good. She washed us clean and prepared our beds very nicely".

Then the woman went to the mouth of the den and asked the frogs, "Did you have a good maid?"

"Yes, she was so good", said the frogs "that we've never before had anyone so good. She washed us thoroughly and even cleaned the walls of our den".

The old woman then went into the house to thank her excellent maid and gave her a chest full of gold and beautiful adornments. Whatever she might want, she would always find it in the chest.

On her way back home the girl carried the chest on top of her head. Seeing her approach, the dog barked, "Here she comes, the old man's beautiful daughter with plenty of gold and other adornments of all kinds! There's nothing she lacks!"

The stepmother got angry with the dog and kicked it with her heel. "What are you barking like that for and praising the beauty of that barrel of tar?" When the girl, having returned to her father's house, showed her beautiful treasure, the stepmother got very angry and would have thrown the chest into the fire had she had the strength to lift it from the ground. Then she said, "Never mind, I'll see to it that my own daughters will be as fortunate!"

The stepmother baked two cakes for her own daughters, and threw the cakes out of the doorway and said to the girls, "Chase after these until they stop—maybe you will find the same fortune!" The cakes rolled down the road, and the girls skipped after them. Then they met a man.

"Pat my head, girls!"

"We're not going to start patting your scabby old head and dirty our hands. Why, the king's son would hardly want us after that, would he?!"

When the cakes stopped at the old woman's cottage, the girls asked for work.

"If you behave yourselves, I'll give you work. But if you don't, I shall reward you with evil".

The old woman told them to go and feed her cows and give them a good drink. The girls went off and threw the fodder at the cows' backsides and knocked the water-troughs over. They then struck the cows' horns with a staff so hard that they came off, and went indoors to ask for the next job. The old woman told them to wash the lizards. The girls went and pulled the lizards' tails off, gouged their eyes and knocked them unconscious. They then went to the old woman again to ask, "Are all the jobs done then?"

The old woman told them to go and clean the

frogs. The girls went and threw dregs over the frogs and said, "What the devil are these kind of creatures good for?" They then went back to the old woman, who said, "Sit yourselves down here for a little while". The old woman went over to the cows and asked, "Did you have good maids?"

"We've never had anybody as useless as those girls! They threw the food at our backsides, poured all the water into the ground and beat us with a staff, so that our horns broke off". Then the old woman went over to the lizards and asked, "Did you have good maids?"

"There's never been anyone as wicked as that; they flung us around the walls. Now our tails are broken, our eyes are gouged, and we're all left for dead". The old woman then went to the frogs and asked, "What did the wicked maids do to you?"

"They filled our mouths and covered our eyes with dregs and even threw small stones at us and asked, 'what are these creatures good for!'"

The old woman went over to the maids and said, "Since you've been such clever maids that we've never had here before, I shall give you this chest as a reward for your troubles". The girls ran off home carrying the chest between them. When they arrived home, the dog barked, "Ooh, ooh, there come the stepmother's daughters carrying fire and tar on their heads!" The stepmother got angry with the dog and wanted to kill it, but the dog managed to run away. When the stepmother opened the chest, she got burnt on the spot as did her daughters.

The old man's daughter married the king's son. And I took my leave.

Tittulas Tuuree

n the back of the woods there stood a humble cottage and there were no children in it apart from one daughter. She was the type of girl who couldn't do any needlework. The king's son happened to be passing by during a hunt and asked, "What is that maiden doing up there on the roof?" The parents answered, "She's spinning gold thread out of straw and clay".

The king's son wondered whether he could have her for his bride, as she seemed to be so clever with her hands. The parents agreed. The prince then took her to the royal court and placed a bale of straw and a bucket of water in a certain chamber and told her to spin gold thread from it.

He waited one day. When the girl hadn't done any spinning on the first day, he ordered that should she not get any work done during the next three days, she'd be put into prison for life. But still the girl hadn't spun anything during those two days. On the evening of the second day she was terribly sad, as there was only one more day left for spinning, and she cried a lot. That evening an old dwarf of a man came to the girl and asked her, "Why are you crying so much?" The maiden said, "I have to be able to spin gold out of that straw and clay in one day or else be sent to prison for the rest of my life".

The dwarf gave the girl a pair of gloves and said, "Whenever you wear these gloves, you'll be able to spin gold. But I'll only let you have them on the condition that you find out my name within three days. If you don't know it by then, I shall take you with me on the evening of the third day".

The gold appeared as promised. But on the third day the maiden grew sad once more. The prince returned from a hunt and asked, "Why are you crying?" But the girl wouldn't say; she just kept crying and was miserable. Then the king's son began to comfort her and said, "What are you crying about? Listen, when I was in the forest I heard an old dwarf dancing around a yew-bush and singing,

> Today the malt is being ground,
> Tomorrow wedding bells will sound!
> The maiden sits and cries in pain,
> For she cannot find out my name.
> Tittulas Tuuree, Tittulas Tuuree I am!

Then the maiden became delighted and stopped crying. The dwarf came to fetch her on the third day and asked, "Now then, do you know my name?" The maiden answered, "Tittulas Tuuree, Tittulas Tuuree!" The dwarf got angry and took his leave, slamming the door behind him. The maiden received the threads of gold and became queen at the king's court.

The Pig Maid

here were three sisters. Two of them had been washing their faces with milk for several weeks, as they were going to work as maids for the king's son. The third one, who always washed her face with water, went along.

They met a sheep, but the two vain sisters would not shear it. The third sister did, and was rewarded with wool.

Then they came to an oven. The two girls would not bake any bread, but the third one did, and was rewarded with a loaf.

Then they came across a beggar. He asked them to stroke his head. The two girls said that they didn't want to dirty their hands since they were on their way to become maids for the king's son. The third girl stroked his head, and was rewarded with a cane. The beggar said, "When you arrive at the king's court, on the left next to the manor, you will see a rock. When you strike the rock three times, a door will open into a room that is full of gold. There you'll find whatever you wish for".

The girl asked if she could look after the king's pigs. She was given a pigskin coat to wear. On Sunday the king's son and the two fine maids went to church. The king's son asked the sisters, "Isn't the pigmaid going to come to church?" After the others had gone, the pigmaid knocked on the rock three times. She then got dressed in gold, took a carriage with two golden horses and travelled at a safe distance so as not to be noticed. She also left the church before the others.

The king's son followed her in his carriage. During the ride, the girl happened to drop some golden bits and pieces. Then she took all her belongings into the rock and sat by the sauna stove wearing her pigskin coat.

The following Sunday they all left for church again. This time the pigmaid dropped a golden shoe on the road. As the king's son was following her, she had no time to remove her golden clothes, but covered them with her pigskin coat. Then the king's son said, "Whoever it was, who came to church dressed in gold and whose foot will fit this shoe, will become my wife".

Everybody tried on the shoe, but it wouldn't fit even though some had cut their toes off with a hooking iron. When the pigmaid tried the shoe, it fitted. She threw off her pigskin coat, stepped down from the sauna bench so that her golden dress made a swishing sound. The king's son took her for his wife, and they had a big wedding.

A Disguised Woman as the King's Brother-in-Law

rmy recruiting had started in the kingdom. And so there was a household where two daughters and one son lived. It fell upon the son to become a soldier, and the elder daughter said, "It's not right at all that we should let our only brother join the army". The other daughter said, "What else can we do, as we have no other brother?"

"There is only one answer; one of us will have to go", said the elder sister. "There's no way that I'm going!" said the younger daughter. "Well, I don't mind going", said the elder sister. "I'll get dressed in my brother's clothes and have my head shorn".

So, she went, and was recruited with no trouble at all, and as she was so pretty and nice, she was chosen to be one of the king's bodyguards. She often had to stand on guard at the king's steps. The king's daughter would often see her, and soon grew very fond of her as she was so beautiful. The daughter said to her father, "Father, could you not promote that soldier to a better position? He is such a handsome and pure man!" "He has not served for long enough yet", said the father, but soon promoted the young man to the officer ranks.

He was again standing on guard at the king's steps. Well, when the daughter saw him dressed in a new uniform that was so grand, he looked more handsome than before; she began to desire him all the more. "Father, could you not promote him to lieutenant-colonel? He is such a pure and handsome man and has not committed a single offence. Promote him to major, please!"

The father promoted the young man to major, but the princess now wanted him to be promoted to the rank of general-in-chief (*sic*). "This is impossible; he has served for such a short time and hasn't even been to war yet", said her father. But his daughter kept insisting and wouldn't give her father any peace. The father said, "It looks as though you want to marry this man!"

"That is exactly what I want!"

The king arranged a magnificent banquet and invited many lords. Well, at the banquet the king made a toast with all the lords. Then it was the turn of the bridegroom to raise his glass to the king, who said, "Cheers, my senior general and son-in-law!" The groom said, "Your merciful majesty, it is not possible as I'm of peasant stock". "There's nothing to be done; my daughter wants you!" said the king. Then they celebrated the young couple's engagement and the wedding followed soon after.

The groom arranged long trips for himself, but all the same, the day arrived when he had to sleep with his wife. "Aren't we going to play any night-games then?" asked the king's daughter. "It wouldn't be proper—we're both alike", answered her husband. The king's daughter grew very sad, and her father noticed it. "Why do you look so sorrowful, even though you won a husband so much to your liking?"

"So much to my liking is he that he's no good for me at all; he's just like me".

"That is unfortunate, indeed", said her father. "What are we to do about it? I think I know—I'll send him abroad to another kingdom, where I have something owing me. I won several thousands of millions in the war". The king then said to his son-in-law, "I'd like you to go abroad and obtain the several thousands of millions which I won in the war".

His son-in-law was very eager to go. That kingdom was so far away that he had to abandon the coach and horses and travel by foot along the coastline. He noticed a man lying on the beach, who had a cannon for a gun which he was pointing out to the sea. "What is your gun pointing at?" asked the son-in-law. "There's a seal over there ten leagues away, I'm going to shoot it!"

"If you shoot it, that's where it's going to stay. Come with me instead, and I'll give you a share of a large sum of money".

The man got up, put the cannon on his shoulders and followed the young man. They walked for a night and a day and met a man who was wearing large chains of iron, and when he struck them together, the forest fell down with a crash. The king's son-in-law said to the man, "Let them fell their forest themselves; come, put your chains on your shoulders. You shall receive a large share of the money from the king whom I'm on my way to now".

The man threw the chains onto his shoulders and joined them. They then came to a vast meadow which they had to cross. When they had reached the middle of the meadow, a man with a wooden leg was approaching from the east and was heading west, with a letter in his hand. The Woodenleg passed them in a flash, then returned in half an hour. The Chainman tripped him with the chains and after catching him, asked, "Where did you go at such a fiery speed?"

"I had to take a letter from one important count to another", he answered.

"Let them take their own letters; if you come with me, you will also receive a share of the large sum of money which is coming to me".

They continued and eventually came to a town which had three windmills on the beach. A man was standing by the windmills, and pressing one nostril down with his thumb and blowing with the other so hard that the windmills were rotating so fast that they nearly took off. The son-in-law said to him, "Come with us! We're on our way to the king; he lives in this town. You too will get a share from the large sum of money".

They continued and soon arrived at the king's castle. When they entered the castle courtyard, the son-in-law left the other men in front of the king's window, while he went inside. The king asked promptly, "What kind of man are you and what is your business?" The young man explained to the king, "I have come for the large sum of money, so and so many millions belong to me". The king said, "Now, my man, you're as good as dead!"

The king, raising himself, looked out of the window and saw the magnificent-looking men standing in the courtyard. The king was startled at the sight of the men and said, "The keys to the kingdom are eighty leagues from here. If you manage to bring them to me within three hours, you shall have the riches you have come for".

The son-in-law went out to ask his men, "Who believes it possible to get the keys of the kingdom in three hours?"

"I'll do it in just two hours!" replied the Woodenleg. The king wrote a letter which was given to the

Woodenleg. The Woodenleg left and soon jumped halfway across the large meadow. Everybody was waiting, and after two hours there was still no sign of him. They went up to the windmill hill and asked the man who had spotted the seal ten leagues away, to look out for the Woodenleg coming back. He looked out and said, "He's sleeping down there on the meadow with a bunch of keys in his hand and a millstone for a pillow".

The king's son-in-law asked the man to load his gun and shoot the millstone from under the Woodenleg's head. The man loaded the gun and shot the millstone, and the Woodenleg woke up. On waking, the Woodenleg sprang up and, bringing the keys, placed them on the table in front of the king, with still half an hour to spare.

The king's son-in-law was then able to collect the money he had been promised. He collected all the gold and silver that he could find in the entire kingdom, even the king's own silver spoons. Soon after, he set sail in the king's finest warship. The Chainman, who was also a seer, said, "The king will gather all his troops and warships and will pursue and imprison us, and take all these possessions back. I can fight well with these chains of mine, but who can hold back a huge force such as this?" The Gunner said, "I can shoot very far with this gun, but who can shoot a fleet of that size?" The Windmill-blower then said, "I can blow a strong headwind, but who can blow the whole sea?" The Woodenleg said, "I can move my bones very fast; in fact, I'm no longer here!"

The next day, as was predicted, many hundreds of warships arrived. The Gunner began shooting. The Woodenleg jumped off the ship and just with one bound landed on dry land, although the distance was several leagues. The Windmill-blower began blowing with one nostril. The king's son-in-law said, "Start blowing with both nostrils!" The man began blowing with both nostrils, and blew so hard that all the warships were driven against the coast and broke into thousands of pieces. Now that peace had returned there was nothing to fear.

They set sail for home. Soon they saw a beautiful island and sailed towards it and cast the ship's anchor by the beach. On that island, there grew all kinds of fruit trees—every variety one could possibly imagine. At the centre of the islet, there stood a hut which was deserted. The king's son-in-law had a call of nature and as the hut was empty, he answered the call right in the middle of the floor.

They then reboarded the ship and set sail for home. The hut happened to belong to a Sámi, and when he returned home from his travels he saw the pile on the floor. "Whoever is responsible for this", exclaimed the Sámi, "will become a woman if he's a man now, but if it's a woman she will become a man!" And so it happened that the king's son-in-law became a man.

They then sailed home to the coast of their own king. The young man had to sleep with the king's daughter, that is, with his own wife. In the morning the daughter said to her father, "Father, everything is all right now! My husband is a real man after all".

The king was very happy now that he had so much gold and silver, and such splendid heroes.

~ ~ ~

The Witch and the Sister of Nine Brothers

nce a wife, who already had nine sons, became pregnant. The sons, fearing that she would have yet another son, ran away, saying to their mother, "If you have a daughter put a spindle above the door, and we'll come back then, but if you have a son put an axe up there, instead". She gave birth to a daughter and put a spindle above the door. But a witch came by at night and replaced the spindle with an axe. When the sons came to check and saw the axe, they never returned.

The daughter grew up, and when her mother told her that her nine brothers had left home because of the witch's deceitfulness, she burst into tears. She caught her tears in a cup, added some flour and made a round cake. Then she went out with her dog and would roll the cake, saying,

Roll, my cake, roll,
Down to my nine brothers
Of one mother!

The same witch sprang over to the girl and said, "I know the way there!" They went, and came to a pond. The witch said, "Let's go and have a swim!" The dog said, "Don't go, she'll deceive you!" The witch kicked the dog, and broke one of its legs.

They carried on walking, the dog hopping along on three legs. Again they came to a lake and the witch said, "Why don't we go for a swim!" The dog said, "Don't go, she'll deceive you!" The witch kicked the dog and broke another leg. They came across two more ponds, and the same thing happened again, so that eventually the dog was forced to roll in order to move along. At the fifth pond the witch kicked the dog and knocked off its head, so that the dog died.

By then, they were approaching the lane where the brothers lived, and the witch said, "Spit into my eyes, and I will spit into yours!" And she kept egging the girl until she spat into her eyes, for the dog was no longer there to warn her. When the witch spat back, she said, "Your looks to me, my looks to you!", as the girl was beautiful and the witch ugly. She even took the girl's tongue and her mind and together they went to meet the brothers. Once there, she told them she was their sister and that she had brought the girl along to be their cowherd. The youths thought all was fine and took the girl for a cowherd.

The witch would always take the girl to the top of the lane and there she would give back her tongue and mind, so that she'd know how to tend to the cows. But on the girl's return, the witch would come back to the lane to take away her tongue and mind. When the witch baked cakes, she always put a stone inside and only a little dough on the outside. While tending to the cattle the girl would sing,

> Hurry day behind the spruce copse,
> Roll down to the birch grove,
> Steal away to the juniper bush,
> Let the cowherd go home.
> The witch is my mistress,
> The wicked wife my ruler,

She bakes my loaves with stones,
With rocks she fills my cakes.
I slash my knife against the stone,
I grate it against the rock,
While tending to
My brothers' herd,
The nine sons of one mother.

The brothers happened to hear the song, went to the girl and asked, "Why do you sing in this way?" The girl told them everything the witch had done. The brothers said, "Go home in the middle of the day, when the witch is not there to meet you, keep your eyes well covered and say they're hurting, and moan a lot".

The witch screamed out, "Why have you come in the middle of the day?" "My eyes are hurting", answered the girl. Then the brothers returned home and said to the witch, "Sister dear, do spit on the s cowherd's eyes so that they would heal!" The witch spat on her eyes, and at the same time the girl said, "Your own looks for yourself, my own looks for myself!" And thus she regained her true form.

Then the brothers heated up the sauna and dug a hole under the threshold which they filled with tar and lit it. Then they covered the hole with a cloth. The witch came up to the door of the sauna but refused to step on to the cloth and said, "First I shall jump on to the stove bench and then on to the higher benches!" But the brothers said, "Step daintily on your tiptoes over the cloth, our one and only sister!" When she did so, she fell into the hole. Thus the witch disappeared, but still screamed while burning,

In my place let there come
Buntings from my eyes,
Magpies out of my hair,
Ravens out of my ears,
Crows out of my toes
To peck the people,
To eat the grain of men!

The Farting Stone

nce there was a young man who was very much in love with the daughter from a nearby house. The girl's parents were against such a union and forbade their daughter ever to marry such a lowly cottage dweller as her suitor. But the suitor was a very resourceful man. He recalled that once a witch had given him a stone which, when one blew on it, caused one to fart a great deal.

At home the boy's beloved would always rise before other folk in order to make coffee. Making a note of this the young man placed his stone quietly under the stove one evening. When the daughter began lighting the fire the next morning and blew on the stone, she was so overcome by a force from the stone that she was unable to blow any more and began to let off rasping farts continuously.

Eventually, when there was no sign of coffee, the mistress of the house came into the kitchen to see what was going on. Here she sees her daughter by the stove lighting the fire. After noticing that her daughter kept farting she scolded her and pushed her away from the fire, and then set about lighting it herself. But before long the mistress was overtaken by the same complaint.

Now even the master of the house got up and went into the kitchen. He took his turn at blowing but soon he sounded like his wife and daughter. As they all had fallen prey to such an ailment at the same time they thought that the devil himself had settled in the nest of their house.

For this reason a parson was brought to exorcise the demon. What do you know—even the parson became ill. The parson found himself in a most awkward situation. This is why he announced in his Sunday sermon that he who can cure this parp-parp disease, shall receive half of the parson's annual salary. At the same time the farmer got up and called out in the middle of the sermon, "Whoever can rid me of this parp-parp disease, I shall give him my daughter and my house!" The daughter's suitor happened to be sitting next to the father in the church, and soon asked, "Are you going to keep your word?"

"I will, come what may", he answered.

Now the suitor went over to the house and removed the stone from under the stove. As soon as he had done so, those who had been blowing on the stone got cured.

And so the suitor became a rich man. He received a house and half the parson's salary, and on top of that his beloved became his wife. Well, what could have been better than that?

The Three Doctors

nce there were three doctors travelling together. They stopped at a house and spent the night there. When evening came, a quarrel started about which one of them was the best and the wisest doctor. One said to the second, "I'll remove one of your eyes for the night and put it back in its place in the morning". Then the second doctor said to the third, "I'll remove one of your arms for the night and rejoin it back in the morning". And finally the third doctor said to the first, "I'll remove your heart for the night and replace it in the morning".

So, they did as they said: one removed an eye, the second removed an arm and the third removed the heart. But during the night, while they slept, the arm was stolen, a cat ate the heart and the eye got lost. When they got up in the morning the doctor who had removed the eye from the second one began searching for it, but couldn't find it. So he went out into the yard, caught the cat and took one of its eyes. He then went back indoors and fixed it to the head of the doctor with the missing eye.

The doctor who had removed the arm from the third one began searching for the arm but could not find it anywhere, as it had been stolen. An old man in the same house had died during the night, so the doctor went up and cut his arm off and then fixed it to the shoulder of the doctor from whom he had removed it.

The third doctor who had removed the heart from

the first one spent the whole morning looking for the heart but was unable to find it, as the cat had eaten it during the night. But some pigs had been slaughtered in the morning. So he went and took one pig's heart and attached it to the doctor with the missing heart.

The doctors asked the one whose eye had been taken out for the night, "Can you see with that eye now?" "It would otherwise be just fine, but I can see with it however dark it gets and it keeps leering at the mice," he answered.

"But surely it's a good thing to be able to see in the dark," added the others.

Then the doctors turned to the one whose arm had been removed for the night. "Does your arm feel well fixed?" To which he answered, "It's been fixed back well enough but it feels as if its an arm of a dead man; it has no strength or sign of life".

Then the doctors asked the one whose heart had been removed for the night, "And how about your heart?" "Well, it would be fine but it's given me a huge appetite; I can't stop eating".

The others replied, "But it must be a good thing to enjoy one's food".

After this the doctors got to keep their respective body parts for the rest of their lives. One of them chased after mice all night long, the second was never able to do any work with his other arm, while the third doctor ate everything he could find.

~ ~ ~

The Cat Child

There was a king who lived happily with his wife and daughter, but the Grim Reaper killed the mother, leaving her spouse and daughter deep in grief. The king did not wish to live unmarried, so he remarried and got a wicked woman for his wife. The wicked stepmother hated the king's daughter and was at a loss as to which evil deed she could commit against this virtuous and beautiful daughter. The princess was engaged to a certain young king, but the evil step-mother didn't want such happiness for the girl. So she enchanted the girl pregnant, for she knew that there was nothing more evil than to do such a thing to a virgin.

Then the wicked woman told the king that his daughter was pregnant. The king became very angry with his daughter and banished her from the castle and forbade her ever to come before his eyes again. The king's daughter left crying, not knowing where to go. She walked a long way and eventually came to a sea shore, where there was a sauna. It was surrounded by a wild, green meadow and there was a spring nearby. The sauna became her home, and in that spring she would look at her own reflection and saw how it became uglier by the day. She kept away from other folk's houses since she had grown so ugly.

She then gave birth to a cat in the sauna and was going to close the door on it straight away, but the cat prayed, "Don't, mother dear, kill me before I've had the chance to make you happy!" The mother let it live.

Soon the cat went off to find work and food for its mother. The cat sat on a piece of spruce bark and, steering with its tail, rowed over the sea to the manor of the young king. The cat asked the king's mother for some food and work. The king's mother thought, "What might your mother be able to do?", but gave it some anyway. The cat took the needlework in its teeth and sat on the spruce bark and, steering with its tail, rowed back to the home shore.

Soon the needlework was finished and the cat took it to the castle. The work had been completed so skilfully that the queen mother was in awe. Now, when the cat asked for more food and work for its mother, it was given better sewing to do. When the cat sat on the spruce bark and was on its way, the king followed it in a boat without the cat noticing.

The king watched where the cat was going, and as it went into the sauna, the king stayed outside and noticed a ring on the windowsill of the sauna, while the king's daughter was bathing. The king took the ring and went away. After she had finished bathing, she saw that her ring had been stolen. She grieved and felt great sadness at its loss, as she didn't know who had taken it. The ring was her only property and now, even it had gone. She cried as she sewed, but this work was better than the first one, which was why she made it very beautiful.

When the needlework was finished, the cat sat on the spruce bark and took it to the castle. When it arrived with the sewing, the king's mother wondered again who was the clever needlewoman and said, "It would be good to have such a clever seamstress in the castle". When the cat asked again for some food and work for its mother, the king's mother told her son to bring the seamstress to the castle.

The king went by boat to fetch her, and the cat went ahead on the spruce bark. When he came into the sauna, the king's daughter recognised her fiance and gladly went with him to the castle. The cat followed on the spruce bark. On their arrival at the castle, the princess regained her previous beauty. The king fell in love with her again, and the mother didn't wish to stand in the way of the marriage. So the king celebrated a wedding with his princess.

After the wedding, the cat said to its mother, "Close the door on me now!" But her mother could not bring herself to do such a thing to the cat who had been so good to her. But the cat kept on insisting, and when its mother still didn't want to kill it, the cat got very cross and scratched so badly that the mother had no choice but to close the door on it. When she had done so, the cat disappeared completely, and the mother didn't know where it had gone to. Every corner was searched, but it was never seen again. Yet the cat had brought its mother great happiness, and the king loved her.

So the king and his wife lived happily ever after, and the witch could no longer do them any harm, which annoyed her a great deal. The wicked witch was then put into a spiked barrel and rolled up and down the hill until she was dead. The witch couldn't get out of the spiked barrel, even though she tried all her magic tricks. And that's how the power of the witch came to an end.

The King's Son on his Way to Marry

nce upon a time there was a queen, who was told, "Your son will be killed on his way to marry". "It would be better", said the queen, "if we were to kill him ourselves". She then gave her son a drink before leaving. The boy's servant was a seer and he advised the boy to throw the drink over his left shoulder. The boy did this and put the empty glass to his lips so that the queen didn't notice. Some drops had fallen into the horse's dish, and after they rode a short while the horse collapsed and died. Three ravens flew to the horse's carcass and on eating it they also died. The boy and his servant took the ravens with them to the castle of the giants, and asked, "May we cook our doves here?" "Yes, you may, as long as you give some to us as well", they said. There were twelve giants in the castle, and they all ate the roasted ravens and promptly died.

The boy and the seer then left the castle. By the road there was a church where every passer-by wrote his name on the door. These travellers did likewise and went inside. There they tore a page from an old book and stuffed it into a gun as a stopper, then fired a shot, and the church caught fire.

Now they arrived at a king's court and went up to the king to ask for his daughter's hand. The king said, "Give the girl three riddles: if she solves them, you shall not have her; if she doesn't, you shall".

The boy said first, "When we set out, little killed

large, large killed three little ones, and the three little ones killed twelve large ones". For the second riddle, he said, "The Lord's word burnt down the Lord's temple". The girl couldn't solve these riddles.

As there was no other way to solve the riddles, one of the king's daughters had to sleep with the boy. The boy told the girl to undress until she was quite naked, and the girl did so. The servant called out to the boy, "The horses are fighting in the stables!", and the boy had to go there and he took the girl's shirt with him.

The next night, another daughter came to sleep next to him in order to find out the answers from the boy. Again, he asked the girl to take all her clothes off and leave her shirt aside. The servant came again and said, "The horses are fighting in the stables!", and the boy rushed over to the stables again and took the shirt with him.

On the third night the king's wife herself went to find out about the riddles. And again the same thing happened, and the boy now even had the shirt of the king's wife.

The king then wanted to understand the riddles, as no one else seemed to. The boy then said, "When I left home, I was given a drink for the road; I threw it over my left shoulder and some drops happened to land on the horse's dish, and the horse died. Three ravens came to pick at the carcass and died on the spot. We then took the ravens and cooked them in the castle of the giants. The giants ate them and died. That was the first riddle. Then we stopped at a church and there was a bible in the pulpit. We tore a page from the bible and stuck it into the gun as a stopper. We then fired a shot, and the church caught fire. That was the second riddle".

Then the king asked, "And what is your third riddle?" The boy replied, "I spent a night at a king's court, and the following night a lynx came to lie beside me; I skinned it, and there you see its skin". At the same time he threw the girl's shirt. "The following night an otter came to me, and I skinned it, and there you see the skin!" Now he threw the other daughter's shirt down. "The third night a crow came to lie beside me; I skinned it and this here is the skin!" He then threw the queen's shirt to the floor.

Then the king said, "I can tell that you have indeed been very close to them—you shall have my daughter".

The Clever Girl at the Inn

The emperor was cunningly trying to find out how wise his generals were, or how good their reasoning was. The emperor had a really large stone by his window, a very large stone indeed. "I'd like you to skin this stone for my wedding attire!"

"How can we possibly skin a stone?" asked the generals. "If you are not able to do it, I'll put you in prison immediately", said the emperor. "I'll give you enough money and one month to complete the task; but skin the stone you must. And if you cannot do it yourselves, seek the answer from someone who can".

Well, when there are only a couple of days left, the

generals find themselves walking by an inn near their home town; they were still none the wiser as to how they might go about skinning the stone. There is a very beautiful girl at the inn, and she asks these gentlemen, "What are you looking for?"

"We are looking for a stone skinner, and were given a month to do it, and still we haven't managed to find a stone skinner and now the emperor will put us in gaol".

The girl says, "You'll get your stone skinned; there's nothing to worry about. When you go back to the emperor, tell him, 'If the emperor would be good enough to start skinning the stone himself, as it is such a precious skin and it would be such a shame to spoil it, if you make a start, we'll finish the job'. And there's no need to say who told you so". So, this is what the generals told the emperor.

"Who gave you this advice?" asked the emperor. The generals didn't want to say. The emperor said, "I'll put you in jail, if you don't tell me!" So they told him that in the last inn they called at, there was a girl who told them what to do. The emperor asked, "Is she a beautiful girl?" They told him that she was beautiful.

Then he gives the generals half a metre of silk thread and tells them to take it to the girl, since she's so clever, let her make a wedding attire for the emperor from it—the emperor was a bachelor, you see.

Well, the generals then take the silk thread to the girl and say, "This can't be enough for the emperor's wedding attire; now it's a trip to gaol for all of us". The girl said, "No need for that, this will do and what's more, there'll even be half left over, which I'll give back to the emperor".

105

Then the girl gave the generals a stick which was half a finger in length and told them to say to the emperor, "Would the emperor kindly make a hand loom from this stick; the girl then will weave the wedding attire from the silk thread".

When they had taken it to the emperor and told him this, the emperor says, "Well, she's clever that girl, isn't she? Go to her and tell her to come to the palace, but she musn't come on a horse, nor on foot, nor on a sledge nor without it, nor should she come all dressed nor undressed; if she's still able to do this, I'll take her for my bride".

The generals went back and told this to the girl. "Be ready to receive me; I'll come all right", said the girl. And she took a large laundry bowl, placed it on the wagon shafts, took a hound and harnessed it, got dressed in nets and drove in front of the palace. The emperor is looking from a hiding place to see just how the girl would arrive.

The girl tied the hound in front of the gate and began climbing up the steps. The emperor burst into laughter, and ran over to greet her, saying, "Now I'll take you for my bride!" And so the emperor took the girl for his bride and said, "You musn't interfere in my affairs, whatever I do; if you interfere, I'll turn you out".

Two farmers live near the emperor. One has a gelding and the other has a mare; and the mare has a foal in the forest. It was summertime; the poor man owned the mare and the rich man the gelding, and when the foal grew stronger, it started to follow the gelding. The rich man said, "My gelding must have had a foal, as it's following him". The poor man said, "That can't be, the foal belongs to my mare".

And so the matter was taken to court and, as the

rich man had bribed the judge, the foal was given to the rich man because it follows his gelding. The poor man then turned to the Court of Appeal where it was decided that the foal should go to the rich man, as it followed his gelding, and the district court had so decided. The poor man wasn't satisfied and appealed to the Senate. In the Senate it was deemed that since an earlier decision had been in favour of the rich man and as the foal always follows the gelding, then it may, indeed, belong to the gelding. Then the poor man takes his papers and his foal to the emperor. Well, the emperor examines the case.

"This has been ruled over many times; there's nothing I can do. Since the foal follows the gelding, it might well be the gelding's offspring". The empress springs up and says, "What kind of an emperor are you! A gelding cannot give birth to a foal; I rule that the poor man gets the foal, the foal was born to the mare, not to the gelding!" And the empress gave the poor man permission to take the foal away, and so he did.

The emperor said to the empress, "Now we'll have a divorce; you went against my word, so you'd better take your leave!" The empress says, "Will you still let me take something, now that you're turning me out?" The emperor said, "Take whatever you may fancy!" The empress says, "I shall take two of the best horses, a golden sledge, an old driver and a carriage, and one more thing".

The emperor agreed and told the empress to leave for another kingdom. And all the dignitaries were invited to the leaving celebrations where they all ate and drank plenty, and the emperor became very drunk. Now that they're leaving, the empress orders the horses to be harnessed. She says, "I'll take one more thing as I've been promised", and takes the emperor and leads him to the carriage. As they're driving through the town, the emperor begins to sober up.

"Where are you taking me?"

"To another kingdom", says the empress, "as you made your promise".

"I did no such thing", says the emperor.

"But your signature stands", says the empress. "Take whatever you fancy—and I fancied you the best and took you".

The emperor says, "Drive back home; now I'll never want to part from you!" And so they returned home and lived happily ever after.

⌣ ⌣ ⌣

Half a Man and a Horse's Head

n the days when Finland was under Swedish rule, the king came to look over this land, travelling on horseback along the highway. By the roadside there was a blacksmith's workshop where a small boy was forging iron. The king rode his horse so close to the workshop that the horse's head popped through the doorway. The king asked, "What is the man forging?"

"But there's only half a man and a horse's head in here", replied the boy. The king became a little flustered by the boy's cheeky reply, but still asked, "Well, haven't you got anybody else here or are you all alone?"

"I do have a mother and a father, a sister and a brother".

"Where are they and what do they do?" said the king again. The boy answered, "My brother's hunting; he'll bring home the bird which he can't catch, but the bird he catches, he releases into the woods".

"What does your sister do?"

"She's crying over last year's laughter", said the boy.

"Where's your father?"

"Burning the firewood burnt last year", said the boy.

"Where's your mother?"

"Baking last year's baked bread", replied the boy.

The king couldn't make head or tail out of these answers, and couldn't decide whether the boy was clever or a fool. But when the king was leaving, he said to the boy, "You must come to the inn to see me: neither at night nor in the daytime, neither naked nor clad, neither on horse nor by foot, neither along the road nor beside it".

When the boy heard this he thought how he should go about it. He braced himself, however, and threw off his clothes; then got clad in some netting. The boy harnessed a billy-goat to the sledge and rode off along the verge and arrived at the inn where the king was, just as the first ray of the sun became visible.

The king asked the boy, "What were those anecdotes you were telling me yesterday? What did it mean when you said that your brother was in the woods and would bring home the bird he couldn't catch, but the bird he could catch he'd throw away into the woods; what kind of a hunter is your brother?" The boy answered, "My brother was on the headland hunting for lice in his trousers. The louse which he was able to catch, he killed and threw into the woods, but those he couldn't catch he brought home with him".

"Well, what was it then that made your sister cry over last years laughter?"

"Last year my sister was playing with the boys; now she's having little ones", said the boy.

"How was it when you said your father was burning the firewood burnt last year?" said the king again.

"Last year my father burnt the unburnt places with sticks of firewood; now he's burning the remainders for charcoal".

"How come your mother was baking last year's baked bread?"

"Last year my mother borrowed some bread, so now she's gone to pay it back".

The king was so delighted with the boy's clever answers that he gave the lad a large sum of money and said, "I have never met such a wise one amongst the uneducated peasant children, and you must become even wiser". And so it happened that with the passage of time the boy grew up and became a close counsellor to the king.

⌒⌒ ⌒⌒ ⌒⌒

The Farmer's Weather Prediction

Now, once there was a king and a farmer. The farmer's field and meadow were placed on the slope of the king's castle in such a way that the farmer always had to pass through the castle courtyard in order to reach his land. So once again the farmer was on his way to gather some hay with his horse from his meadow. On his way back the king happened to be in the courtyard of his castle and, seeing the hay load, said to the farmer, "You fool! How dare you drive your hay load through my courtyard! Aren't you ashamed of yourself!"

"I beg your pardon, my merciful king", said the farmer, "but it's the circumstances that forced me to drive through here, as there will soon be thunder and heavy rainfall, thus all my hay would've got soaked through. To go round the castle would have taken too long and I wouldn't have been able to finish before the rainfall; that's why I've hurried home through here".

"Rain?" asked the king, "How do you know that?"

"Well, I know it, merciful father of our land", said the farmer, "from the fact that those gadflies are trying to get under my mare's tail, and that's a sure sign of rain".

"I see", said the king and told the man to leave.

And soon the king went over to his royal observatory, and the almanac writer took his long tube* and

*Telescope

111

looked through it, studied the sky and said, "No, my lord king, there won't be any rain today, tomorrow, or even the day after tomorrow, not even the size of a tear drop, but only after that there may be some rain".

"I see, I see", said the king and left the observatory and went back into the castle. Alas, on the way from the tower, before he had time to get to the castle, such thunder and heavy downpour started and didn't stop for a whole hour, that the king became very frightened indeed, and was so completely soaked through like a white poodle after swimming in the stream. Now the king arrived back at the castle, feeling really cold, ordered the almanac writer to be brought before him and said, "You tube-starer*, you've lost your job since you know nothing about weather. Even a stupid bumpkin of a farmer knows by looking under his mare's tail, when it'll rain and when it'll shine!" And so the king removed the almanac writer from his post and made him clear the manure instead.

The king then ordered the farmer to be brought before him and gave him the entire observatory to live in, the title of an astronomer together with the annual salary that used to be paid to the almanac writer. And thus the farmer became the king's friend to the annoyance of all the lords at the castle, and entirely with the help of the gadflies and horseflies.

And that's all.

*Astronomer

The Sailor and the Parson

The parson asked the sailor, "What sort of man was your grandfather?"

"He was a sailor, like me".

"Is he still alive?"

"No, he's already dead".

"How did he die?"

"He drowned in the sea".

"What sort of man was your father?"

"He was also a sailor".

"Where did he die then?"

"He died at sea".

"Weren't you afraid to go to sea, where all your forefathers have died?"

The sailor asked the parson, "What did your grandfather do for a living?"

"He was also a parson".

"Is he still alive?"

"No, he's already dead".

"Where did he die?"

"He died peacefully at home in his own bed".

"What did your father do for a living?"

"He, too, was a parson".

"And is he still alive?"

"No, he's dead already".

"Where did he die then?"

"At home peacefully in his bed".

"Well, aren't you afraid to rest in your bed, where all your forefathers have died?"

The Merchant's Son Casts his Net

nce upon a time there were two merchants. One had a daughter, and the other had a son. Then the merchant who had a son became poor and he had to send his son out begging. The boy even called at the rich merchant's house, where he was always given plenty. The daughter of the house said to her mother, "Mother, why do you give more to that boy than to the other beggars?" The mother answered, "Had his father stayed rich, the two of you would have become one".

The girl began to think that they could still become one. The rich merchant had many ships ready to sail overseas. The daughter was invited to the harbour to see them sail off. But she wouldn't go and stayed behind collecting money for the boy. She then invited him to the house and said, "Mother told me that we would have become a couple if you'd still been rich. Sail overseas now and gather up some possessions. Then return to me; I'll wait seven years for you".

Well, the boy sailed abroad and managed to acquire plenty of property, but he then began playing cards with gentlemen and lost everything. More than seven years had passed and he should have returned home. But now he didn't even have enough money for the fare home. The girl was still waiting for him. She was visited by many suitors and as there was no sign of the boy she felt that he would not be returning, and agreed to marry a sea captain.

The boy was much aggrieved in the foreign lands and went to a forest to cry. An old man came by and asked, "Why are you crying, my lad?" The boy told the old man the whole story—what had happened in his life and how he'd come to lose his entire fortune. The man then gave the boy a gold coin and said, "Take this coin; go and gamble with it and you'll win your fortune back".

But the boy was hungry and used the coin to buy food. He returned to the forest crying, and the same old man came by and said, "Why are crying, my lad?" Again the boy told everything and how he'd bought some food with the coin. This time the old man gave him two gold coins and said, "However hungry you may be, you must use these coins for a gamble and you'll win back all you've lost and even what your opponent owns".

The boy did as was told and won his opponent's twelve fully-loaded ships, which were just then about to sail for the town where his bride lived. He had even won the gentleman's house and all his property—plenty of silver and gold. The boy gave the house back though, but kept everything else, and set off for his hometown.

Just then a wedding was taking place, and the boy arrived at the house as a sailor and asked for some water for washing. He gave the maid a gold coin and said, "Ask the bride to come over for a chat!" But the bride wouldn't come. The boy gave more money and said, "At least try to arrange it!" Eventually the bride came downstairs to the boy, but did not recognise him. Then the wedding guests came downstairs to see who was it who wished to speak with the bride, and the bride said to the boy, "Oh dear, what will become of me, when my bridegroom will see me with a strange man!"

"Go and hide under the bed, I'll cover you with a

blanket", said the boy. Then the wedding guests came and asked him about his travels and other things. The boy said, "Seven years ago I cast my net on this shore and now I've come to raise it". They all laughed—for who'd be such a fool as to come and raise his nets after such a long time!

"If you gentlemen wish to see how it's done, then I'll show you", said the boy. He lifted the blanket, and there was the daughter in her wedding gown with a crown in her hand. The bridegroom became very angry, as did the whole household when the daughter had brought such shame in allowing a strange man to hide her under the blanket. The wedding celebrations came to an end, the bride was stripped off her gown and dressed in old rags instead, and was driven out of her home.

The boy then said to the girl, "Since you've been treated so badly on my account, I will arrange a good position for you as a maid. Come with me to the shore!" The girl went, and when they got onto the ship the boy said, "I am the one whom you sent overseas, and all these ships belong to me now!" He then dressed her in gold and silver, and told his seamen to cover the street all the way up to her house with a fine cloth, the sort that is used for the parade uniforms of the military officers. The boy then led his bride along the covered pavement to her home, where their wedding was celebrated. Even I was there, and what a splendid piece of merry-making it was!

The Prophecy of Murder and Incest

nce upon a time two sages were wandering round the world. One evening they came to an inn and asked for a bed for the night but as they were travelling by Shank's pony, the inn-keeper wouldn't give them a room. Instead, he put them up in the bakery for the night. The sages climbed on top of the oven to sleep, and very pleasant it was to rest in the bakery which was still warm after the day's baking.

In the night, heavy groaning could be heard from the room next to the bakery, as the innkeeper's wife was giving birth. From the cowshed, also, one could hear the sorry bleating of the sheep, and the younger sage asked his friend, "Who's that bleating in the cowshed?"

"A sheep is giving birth to a lamb and is bleating in labour pangs", said the elder sage. "Won't you help it, so that it needn't suffer so much?", pleaded the younger one. "It's of no use, as a wolf will come and eat both the ewe and the lamb in any case", said the elder sage. "Let it eat them later, but just help them now, please!" So the elder sage helped the ewe, and the lamb was born.

The inn-keeper had overheard the travellers' talk, and thought to himself that it was indeed miraculous that they had prior knowledge of the wolf's meals.

The younger sage turned to the elder one again and asked, "Who's that groaning in the bedroom?" "It's the inn-keeper's wife, she's having little ones", replied the elder sage.

"Help her, so that she wouldn't groan so much!"

"It wouldn't be proper, really. Both mother and son should be left to die, thus grave sins would be prevented".

"What kind of sins would be prevented?" asked the younger one.

"Murder and incest", said the elder one.

"And how would these sins come about then?" asked the younger one again.

"The son who's about to be born will kill his father and marry his mother", said the elder sage.

"Come what may, just help the mother now!" pleaded the younger one. So the elder sage let the child be born—it was a boy.

The inn-keeper had overheard this conservation also and began to wonder how could this all be prevented, so that the sage's prophecy wouldn't come true. When the boy was baptised there was a big celebration, all kinds of food, including roast lamb. When the roast was ready, it was put on the window sill to cool down, and since it was winter, the wolves were very hungry and brave, and one came to the window and took the roast and ate it. When the servants came to take the roast to the table, they looked out of the window and saw the wolf gnawing the last bit of the ewe's leg.

The inn-keeper became frightened when he realised that the second prophecy had come true. He pondered how to prevent yet another. In the spring he took his son to the river and threw the baby, nappy and all, into the river and thought that the boy would not now come to kill him, and marry his mother.

The baby drifted along the river for many kilometres. There was a gentleman rowing his boat in the river who spotted the boy floating down the river; the baby's clothes had prevented him from sinking. The man took the baby home with him, and reared him until he was eighteen years old. The boy had a black mark, shaped like an arrow, on his chest. It was impossible to remove the mark; it looked as if it had been there from birth.

The gentleman died, and the boy had to leave the house. He went to look for a job as a groom and eventually arrived at his old home. There his mother still lived—a beautiful, plump mistress who had not aged at all and still looked like a girl in her twenties. She told the boy that there was a groom's position available, as the inn-keeper was getting old and could no longer do all the work. The master hadn't returned from the forest yet, so the boy had to await his decision.

The evening came but there was no sign of the inn-keeper. There had been some thieves in the storehouse and the mistress said that the boy could stay the night and keep watch with a gun and shoot any thieves that he may see breaking into the storehouse. It was a beautiful, moonlit winter's night.

When the one who intended to be a groom had been on watch a short while, he saw a man, carrying a handspike on his shoulder, come from the forest and put something under the door of the storehouse. While doing this, he got down on all fours at the base of the storehouse. The boy thought that this man must surely be a thief, and so he took a shot at him, and the man died on the spot.

The boy went to tell the mistress that the thief was now dead, and then, together they went to have a look, to see who the thief might have been. The mistress soon realised that it was her husband who had just brought her a piece of wood for a new spatula and was about to push it through the cat-flap in the door of the storehouse. She began sobbing dreadfully now that the inn-keeper was dead, and he wouldn't get any better now that he was lying there quite lifeless. She consoled herself with the thought that he was an old man already, and that he would not have lived much longer anyway.

The groom then began spending more time at the inn and eventually the widow grew fond of him, and they lived like any other couple, sleeping together in the same bed. Once in the sauna the mistress noticed the mark on the boy's chest and asked where it had come from. The boy told her that he had had it from birth, and also that a gentleman had found him in the river as a baby. The mistress then realised that this was her own son, and recalled what the sages had predicted and now had come true.

They were both struck with a great worry and decided to go to the parson and told him what had happened. The parson also became very worried and soon wrote to the bishop asking for advice. The bishop called a ministerial convention, and after three months in sitting, it was decided that the boy had to carry water in a sieve from the spring to the roots of an old pitchy stump, and the mother, holding a black sheep, should stay by and pray until the pitchy stump grew leaves and the black sheep turned white.

The boy began to carry water in the sieve to the roots of the pitchy stump, and the mother sat by, and twelve years passed in carrying water but not a single leaf emerged.

Once a year a fat dean would walk down this road

and always had a large sack of money in his cart. He would always laugh and mock the son who, with his mother, was toiling away for nothing. As this was the twelfth time that the dean passed by, the son, in great anger, killed the dean. Now when he carried water to the roots, the stump sprang out leaves and the black sheep turned white.

The son went with his mother to the parson and told him that the stump had grown leaves and the black sheep had turned white. The parson was much bemused by this as there were still three years of penitence left, and was now wondering which good deed had been accomplished for the Lord. The boy said he hadn't done any good deeds, but on the contrary, had committed another crime on top of the first one; he had killed the dean, and soon after that the stump had grown leaves, and the sheep had turned white.

The parson said that killing the dean had been the good deed, as he always collected the parsons' salaries and, yet, never did any preaching himself.

⌣ ⌣ ⌣

The Stonemason's Apprentice as a Bank Robber

The king had a son, and as he was such a heavy drinker, the king lost his patience. "You can go to the gallows", said the king, "before my very eyes!" With a knapsack on his shoulders, the prince set off on his travels out into the wide world, and came to a town called Hirsipuu.* Soon after arriving he went to an inn for some refreshment. There he met a stonemason who was building a bank—the king's new bank. Sitting at the same table, the stonemason asks the traveller, "What kind of craftsman are you?"

"I'm a stonemason's apprentice", he answered.

"I'm a master stonemason myself and I've just been given the job of building the king's bank", he replied. "Come, I'll take you on", he continued.

"All right", he answered.

"I will give you free lodgings and as you seem to be a clean living man, you can stay at my house".

The next morning all the men arrived for work. The master and the apprentice were working opposite each other—one was on the inside, the other on the outside. The apprentice worked on the windows, as right from the beginning he had had the intention of getting into the bank. Soon the bank was ready, and the money was put inside.

The apprentice stayed on at his master's house.

---

*Gallows.

They had a good time and drank a lot. Soon the master ran out of money. "Now I'm flat broke", said the master to the apprentice. "Not to worry, there'll be more money", answered the apprentice.

Well, the apprentice went to rob the bank and took a large sum of money from there. The gentlemen at the bank had carefully counted the money and when they went to count again, a large sum was missing, as the apprentice had stolen hundreds and thousands. So they had a thorough investigation to find out how the robber had got in. All the doors were locked, but the lock on the bank safe was broken.

After a while, the king placed a pair of scissors into the safe in such a way that they would thrust out into the robber's throat when the safe was opened. "The robber is bound to return for more. He wouldn't do it just the once", said the gentlemen.

When the money ran out, the apprentice said to the master that they should go and get some more. This they did, and the apprentice told the master to go before him through the secret hatch into the bank. Well, he stayed there a long time, and the apprentice thought that the master might take it all and not leave him any. The apprentice then decided to go in and saw the master lying on the floor with his throat cut. He had to hurry to take the money and his master's head, leaving the body behind as it would have been too difficult to carry. He had to remove the head so that the body wouldn't be identified. On returning home he told the master's wife what had happened. "Here's the head, but I had to leave the body behind. There's plenty of money now, so you've nothing to worry about, it'll last you for the rest of your life", said the apprentice.

At ten o'clock the next morning the gentlemen

went to the bank. All the doors were still locked just the way they had been left. It was strange to find a body there without a head and all the doors locked. The king was informed that a robbery had taken place for the second time and that this time a headless body was left behind.

The body was taken through the streets in a cart. Up one and down the other, and the police were supposed to notice who the relations were by the sorry sound they would hear, go to where the sound is coming from and arrest them.

Well, the body is carried down the street past the mason's window. The apprentice said, "Come and have a look, your late husband is being carted around!" When the wife saw this, she cried out loud and fainted. Soon the police rushed in hearing where the sound was coming from. Noticing this the apprentice cut his finger with a penknife, so that blood gushed out.

"What's all this noise? You must be related to the body?" asked the police. "Oh, it's nothing", said the apprentice, "I just cut my finger, and my wife, seeing what I had done, fainted". The police, thinking this to be the case, left. So they were none the wiser on this occasion.

"Now there's nothing else for it", said the king, "but for the corpse to be taken from the town up to the hill and hung with a rope from the tree. Surely his relatives will come and take his body away".

Twelve soldiers came to stand guard, in case anyone came to take the body away. The apprentice guessed that this might happen. He went to the tailor and bought twelve bishops' robes. He then went up the hill where the body was hanging, and it was such a slushy day, just snow and water. "What on earth are you doing here", he said to the soldiers, "in such dreadful weather?"

"We are on guard so that nobody can come and steal the body. If anyone does, we'll catch them".

"Well", said the apprentice, "I guess you could do with a drink now".

"Oh yes", replied the soldiers, "but where can we get one?"

"I have some", said the apprentice. "There's enough for each man".

They eagerly took the drink and were very grateful to the man for warming them up. The spirit had been mixed with a sleeping draught and the guards fell asleep. The apprentice undressed the soldiers and clothed them in the bishops' robes. The soldiers just slept and knew nothing of what was going on. The apprentice then took the body down from the tree and buried it together with its head.

When the guards woke up in the morning, they noticed that they were all dressed as bishops, and the corpse was no longer hanging from the tree. They said it must have been the same young rascal who gave them the drinks and had removed the corpse. Well, there was nothing to it but to go to the king dressed as bishops. The king saw the twelve bishops arrive from his window—so many bishops in his kingdom! He didn't know what to expect now that the bishops were on the attack, and said to his wife, "I suppose they're coming to damn me because I let the corpse be hanged from the tree".

Both parties—the king and the soldiers—feared the meeting. When the soldiers had arrived, the king, feeling very worried and not knowing what the bishops might do, came downstairs. But the bishops prayed for forgiveness. "I see", said the king. "It looks like it's the one and the same joker who has robbed the bank!"

The king was wondering how to catch the bank robber. He arranged a big banquet at the court inviting all the gentlemen, both single and married. The king said to his daughter, "When it's time to retire, leave the door to your bedchamber open". All the gentlemen had plenty to drink, and the king gave some black ink to his daughter. "Let him into your bed", said the king. "I'm sure it will be that same rascal again, and draw a cross on his forehead so we'll know in the morning who it was".

The apprentice also attended the banquet. During the night when all the gentlemen were asleep, the apprentice, with mischief on his mind, went to the princess's bedchamber and lay beside her. The princess drew a cross on his forehead without him noticing. When he got up, he looked in the mirror. He saw the sign on his forehead and thought, "Oh dear, they've got their boy now!" He went back to the princess's bedchamber and found the inkwell by the bed. He then went to every room and drew the same sign as he had on the forehead of each sleeping man. After that he retired peacefully to bed.

The next morning, when everyone had got up, the king came to have a look at his guests, to see who had the sign. They all had it. The king went over to his daughter, "You're quite a whore; you've slept with everybody, whether married or single! They all have the sign on their foreheads!"

The daughter said that she drew the cross on one man only. "Well well, this man is impossible to track down. What shall we do now to find out who robbed the bank?" said the king. Flying into a temper, the king then announced in front of the gentlemen, "He, who has robbed the bank, will have my daughter in marriage and may sit on my throne!"

"Well, it was me!" said the apprentice. "Follow me to the bank, all of you, I'll show you how to get in". He led them in through the secret door, which none of the gentlemen had been aware of before.

Well, the apprentice got the princess and sat on the king's throne. The king was greatly annoyed, but could not go back on his word. After some time had passed, the young man produced papers which showed that he, too, was a prince. He took his young wife with him to meet his father in the land where he had come from. "I travelled to the place", said he, "where you had told me to go, and now I'm the king in Hirsipuu, and this here is my wife".

His father, quite astonished, thought that even a drunkard managed to become a man, although he had passed such a heavy sentence on him.

⌣ ⌣ ⌣

The Helsinki Academy

ell, as far as we know, the Academy is such a place that if one should happen to be standing by the entrance steps at twelve noon, then one will never ever get to go anywhere else. There would always be gentlemen standing on guard all day long, so that if anyone happened to be passing by, the gents would seize him and push him into a hot chamber. There he'd be stripped of his clothes and all his money. Then the person would be hung from his jaw on a hook of iron, and the chamber would be heated until it was hotter than hot. The man would faint straight away, and all the flesh and fat would drip down into some dishes which the doctors used for making up medicine. And that is why we country folk never take medicine, as we know for sure what it's made of. The academy will still find men fit for this purpose, but nowadays it's only at the twelfth hour exactly that one can be taken off the steps and at no other time.

Once an old man was taken there against his will. He was very fat and greasy, which pleased the gentlemen no end, as they thought they'd got a good catch. The old man got the same treatment as the others, but he managed to free himself from the hook and took his clothes and with these protected his body from the excessive heat. The old man was also able to breathe in some cold air from the keyhole in order to stay alert till the morning. There was also a big hole in the wall, where all the money taken from the dead was kept. He then filled up his chest with lots of money and found some iron scales in the corner, which he used for striking dead the first to come through the door.

So the old man returned home a very rich man, and I happen to know whose forefather he was, but in the interest of the living descendants, I'll not mention his name.

The Devil Buys Wood

nce upon a time the devil wanted to buy some wood. He came to a house and asked whether there was wood for sale. The farmer agreed to sell some, as the price offered was a good one. He sold the devil all the trees that were neither straight nor crooked. The devil was promised all such trees at the agreed price.

Well, they went to have a look at the wood. The devil flew through the forest, looking here and there and kept calling out, "That one's straight, that one's crooked! That one's straight, that one's crooked!"

Finally the whole forest had been looked over, and the devil didn't get a single twig. He just said, "Oh, you wicked man, the way you've cheated me in buying wood, you've left me with nothing!"

The Unknown Bird

here was a hunter who was very eager to hunt, but somehow never managed to catch any birds. Once in the woods, the devil came to him. "Why do you waste your time walking in the woods since you never catch anything anyway?" said the evil man.

"Desire draws me to it, and it's good to live in

hope", mused the man.

"It'll never come to anything, even if you spent your whole life hunting", said the devil. "But if you make a deal with me, there'll be plenty of birds for you, any kind you want", he continued.

They pondered over the reward, and the devil said, "I won't take any reward for the time being, but if, over a period of one year, you're not able to bring me a bird that I'm unable to identify, I will take you".

The man was satisfied with the deal, and soon he was catching plenty of birds of all kinds. He would often go over to the devil to show his catch, but Judas knew all of them. The end of the year was approaching, and the man began to fear that he might fall into the devil's power.

Eventually the man took his wife and tarred her all over and then rolled her in feathers and took her to the forest. The devil came from the back woods. "What bird is that you've got there?"

"It's over there on the hill", said the man. "Go and have a look. See if you can recognise it yourself", he continued. The devil went over to the woman, but soon came running back and said, "You can keep your bird, my fellow; I don't want to know such a bird! It looked a bit like my wife but had a foul smell and was even more hairy". The man won his bet and became very rich from his hunting.

The Devil Eats his Thingy

nce the devil's son and a farmer set off for the woods, and the farmer had taken a packed lunch with him, whereas the devil's son had none. Well, after a few days in the woods the devil's son got hungry. They stopped and made a campfire, and the farmer had rolled a long sausage out of some meat and was roasting it over the fire. So the devil's son asked, "Where did you get that from?"

"I cut off my thingy and now I'm cooking it".

Now the devil's son said, "Let me have a taste; if it's good, I'll cut off my thingy, too". Well, the farmer let him taste it. The devil's son said, "That is really good; I'll have to cut off my thingy as well!" He took his knife and cut his thingy off; he then put it on a skewer, roasted it and ate it. The devil's son became ill as everything swelled up when he'd cut his thingy off.

After a while they returned home. The farmer's wife was baking bread and her husband said to her, "Quickly, take off your clothes!" The farmer's wife took off her clothes and put her husband's clothes on instead, whereas the farmer put his wife's clothes on. He started baking, and his wife went to bed.

The devil's son had also gone home and was very poorly. His father asked, "What's the matter?" "On the hunting trip I ate my thingy; the farmer had cut his off first", said his son.

The devil's father wouldn't believe that the farmer had cut it off and decided to go and see. When he arrived at the farmer's house, the wife was busy baking the bread—but it was really the farmer—and asked, "Where's your husband?"

"Over there in bed".

"Has he cut his thingy off while hunting?" asked the devil.

"He hasn't said anything".

So he goes over to the farmer himself and asks, "Have you cut your thingy off on your hunting trip?" The farmer's wife replied, "Well, yes I did eat it out of hunger". But the devil wouldn't believe it and said, "Show me then!" The farmer's wife opened her trousers and put her leg onto the side of the bed. The devil had a good look and wondered at what he saw. "Oh, dear, you've even cut your balls off!"

He then went home and gave his son a good hiding. "What are you complaining about, the farmer had even cut his balls off and he isn't ill at all!"

Four Sámi in the Giant's Gorge

There were four Sámi who were looking for food in a woodland gorge, and after some time they spotted some flames rising from another gorge. They headed for the ravine which turned out to be the giant's cave. The giant wasn't at home, but there was a whole ox cooking in a huge pot. The Sámi began to eat the ox and then poured some cold water into the pot and covered it with a lid.

Eventually the giant arrived at the gorge with a great rumble and first of all had a look in the pot, and got so angry that he threw the lid against the silver wall so hard that it got stuck there. Then he got hold of one of the Sámi and put him into the pot, but forgot to light the fire underneath. He then fastened the other three Sámi with iron chains to the wall and threw some earth onto the floor of the gorge while he waited for the meat to get cooked, and fell asleep and snored so that the whole gorge was shaking. The Sámi then came out of the pot and went to the mouth of the gorge to check on his companions.

When the giant woke up and was about to start eating, he noticed that there was nothing in the pot, and became so angry once again that he nailed the pot to the wall. Then he cried because his eyes were hurting and he could hardly see anything. One of the Sámi said that if the giant were to let them free, he would put some ointment in his eyes to make them better, and the giant let them go. The Sámi was melting some lead and told the giant to lie down on his back. When he did so, the Sámi poured the melted lead into the giant's eye, and the giant cried for help and screamed so horribly that it could be heard in the next gorge. When some giants arrived, they asked, "What's the matter with you now?" The giant said, "Nothing is doing wicked things to me!" (the Sámi had told him that his name was Nothing). The other giants got angry because he had fooled them, and left.

Then the giant threw himself at the foot of the gorge in wait for the Sámi and meant to kill them as they'd be leaving the gorge. But the Sámi had skinned the giant's lambs and pulled the skins over themselves as they left the gorge with plenty of gold and silver. As they were leaving the gorge, the giant stroked each of them thinking they were his lambs and lamented, "There goes my dear sweetheart!" And this is how the Sámi were able to escape.

The First Gun

There was once even a time when nothing yet was known of guns. And so it happened in those days that a foreign gentleman was walking here in Finland (meaning the time when the gun was only just invented), and he dropped this strange little thing on the highway.

Two men were walking along this same highway and saw the gun. They couldn't recognise what kind of thing this was but understood that it was just an object, nothing more than an object, and the other one said, "It looks like it's a whistle of a sort, because it has a kind of a hole and a valve, too".

"No way is it a whistle", said the other one. "It's too long for that; I think it's a cracker—an explosive of some kind".

"It's not a cracker at all", the other one answered. "It must be a whistle", he went on. "Get hold of that valve", he told the other, "and pull it, while I blow into the hole".

The other one did as was told, and so the two men began playing this new kind of whistle in tandem. But just as the other one had managed to put the whistle into his mouth while his friend pulled the valve, the gun fired and the first man was thrown backwards onto the ground. His life had also been blown onto the snow, but the other one couldn't believe it, got angry and said, "Oh my, I didn't half get frightened! Didn't I say that it was an explosive?" "What are you pulling faces for, it didn't seem to do you much good either, the way it exploded", he thought.

The bullet had gone right down his friend's mouth and his teeth were caught in a kind of sneer, but the other one thought he was just pulling a face as he'd had such a fright.

The Branch Cutter

A man was walking along the road and saw someone sitting on a branch of a tree, cutting the very branch he was sitting on. The passer-by said, "My good fellow! You'll soon fall down!" Well, he kept walking on, and soon the man who was up in the tree fell down as the branch had broken off. "He'll probably know when I'm going to die, since he knew when I was going to fall off", the man thought. So he went after the passer-by to ask, "Since you knew when I was going to fall, you're bound to know when I'm going to die". The man said, "Yes, I know it all right; when you've farted three times, you'll die".

The man packed his load and headed home, but the load fell off. As he struggled to pull the load up, out came the first fart. Well, he pulled the second time. And let out another one. Well, that got him thinking, "Now my end is near for sure, as there's only one fart to go". He pulled with all his might, fearing that the last fart might escape, but come it did in the end. The man threw himself onto the snow. Well, his horse was standing near, harnessed. Wolves came up and ate the horse. The man said, "You couldn't eat my horse, if I were alive, but as I'm dead, it can't be helped".

The man lay there for a while, dying. Eventually he became hungry and cold, and so had to go home without his horse.

The Bustle of the Numskulls

n the olden days there lived some people known as the numskulls. They didn't have a church and so decided to build one. They built it on the top of an impossibly high hill. When the church was ready, a wise man came by.

"You could have built the church a little lower down the hill and you'd have had less trouble pulling the timber up".

So the numskulls dismantled the church and started building it lower down the hill.

When the church was finished the only opening that was left was for the door. A notice was given that come the first clear day, light was to be gathered into the church; two men from each house with long sacks were to catch the bright sunshine. An awful lot of people with sacks on their shoulders turned up. They would collect some daylight by letting the sun shine into the opening of the sack for a little while and would then fasten the sacks and hurry along to the church. But the church didn't get any lighter. For seven days the numskulls collected more light for the church. Still the church got no brighter. The same wise man happened to come by and said, "It would be much better if you cut some holes into the walls rather than carrying on like a bunch of fools". The numskulls said, "We will do just as you say".

Building was much easier from the top downwards rather than from the bottom upwards. So the numskulls began knocking holes into the church walls and a mighty lot of holes they managed to knock.

After such hard work the numskulls got hot with sweat. They noticed a rippling field of corn nearby and called to each other, "Let's go and have a swim!" They all went swimming in the rye field. On their return one man had apparently drowned, as they'd made a mistake in counting; they'd all excluded themselves in the count. When the wise man turned up again they complained to him, "One of us was drowned in the rye field while swimming!" The wise man counted them all, and all were there—exactly the number they'd said. Feeling happy about this the men went back to work in the church.

The numskulls looked the church over and were pleased with it. The church was good in every way: it had been built at the foot of the hill as the wise man had advised; there was plenty of light now that the walls had been knocked through. Now the numskulls were well pleased.

They then noticed a pine tree which was leaning to one side by the lake, and said, "We have received plenty; now we must help those who are in need". So they congregated round the pine which was tilting towards the lake. They gave it a drink of water, as they thought it was thirsty. But this stubborn, deep-rooted pine tree wouldn't obey readily. They sent out a message, "Gather up plenty of rope! There's a thirsty pine by the lake, that needs to be given a drink!"

An enormous number of men, along with an equally large amount of rope, appeared. They tied a length of rope to the top of the tree and took the other end to the other side of the lake. Then the rest began pulling the ropes, and one man went to the top of the tree to see when it would drink. But the pine wouldn't yield to their pulling and snapped its crown at the same time, taking off the head of the man who'd been watching the pine drink. The reason for this was that the pine had sprung back when they pulled it towards the lake. Those who were behind the lake said to each other, "Humiliation is before us".

They came over to check where the pine had been standing and saw a headless man lying on the shore. The numskulls gave him quite a hiding for not speaking, and said, "Why didn't you call out when the pine was drinking, and we would've stopped pulling before the top of the tree broke!" Well, the headless man gave no answer, and suffered the punishment from the others. The numskulls took their leave and carried the headless man home and said to his wife, "How come you sent your husband out to us without his head?" The wife said, "I didn't forbid him to take his head with him; maybe he's left it in one of his hats". She went to have a look at her husband's hats. She came back and said to the men, "My old man only has three hats: one for church, another for everyday use and a cap for the barn, and I fetched them all. Come and have a look!"

The numskulls inspected the headgear and could not find his head anywhere. The wise man came by and said, "You man-killers! Now you'd better flee your village in a hurry!" And so the numskulls took off on their journey, and I don't have a clue where they've got to.

The Twelve Brothers

Once there was a house in which twelve brothers lived. They had worked very hard indeed and now thought, "Let's go to sell our produce!" They prepared the sleighs and left in the morning. The brothers covered a long distance and it took them all day. When they arrived at a house in the evening, they placed their sleighs by the gate from which they were to set off later. When the farm owner heard of their plan he moved the sleighs during the night over to the same gate that they had arrived at. When they got up in the night and harnessed the horses, they said, "It's nice to start off from here; no need to ask the way".

And so the brothers set off and drove along the road, when one of them said, "Some of these places look just like those we passed yesterday". Another one said, "Places look the same everywhere". They drove on and on. The same one said again, "I bet this is the same road that we travelled along yesterday!" "No, it's not; how could it be, since we put our

141

sleighs at the foot of the road?" said the others.

Again they drove on and by the afternoon they could see a village. One of them said, "Good, there's a village in sight; we'll feed our horses there". Another said, "Looks just like our village!" The others cried, "But there aren't many like our village". And then they recognised it. "It is our village after all!"

So they went home, as nothing had come of their sales trip, and unloaded their goods. In the morning they were wondering, "What shall we do today then, as the sales trip was no good?" Someone said, "Let's go and collect some firewood!" All were satisfied with this. "Right, let's go!"

They only took one horse for this. All day they chopped the firewood while the snow melted off the lake, and they went beyond the lake. In the evening it was time to go home, but the horse wasn't shod and the ice was bare as the snow had melted. "How can we lead the horse now; the ice is too slippery for it?" they said. "Now we'll have to come up with a good idea how to move the horse, as it is unable to stand on ice".

They turned the horse on its side and began pulling it. One of them looked behind. "What could that be, that brown stain left behind?" The skin and the flesh were rubbing off as the animal was being pulled on its side, leaving bloodstains on the ice. One of them said, "Well, I already thought that it might be a good job to put some splints under the animal". "Why didn't you say it before; why wait till now?" they all joined in.

They pulled the horse a while longer up to the river bank, but the horse died. They went into the house feeling angry with one another because the horse got killed in such a way. After a night's sleep, they each went their own way. There was nothing else to divide amongst themselves except thirteen poods* of flour—and there were twelve of them. One pood too many, they realised. "How shall we divide the remainder?"

One suggested, "Let's cook some gruel!" Well, they took it to the frozen lake shore and poured it into the hole in the ice, and said, "We'll eat this together!" They stirred the flour mixture, but it wouldn't thicken. Then one of them said, "I'll bring my pood of flour, as this isn't thickening at all". And so they all went and got their poods of flour and all the flour was thrown into the hole in the ice. But it still wouldn't thicken. Then one of them said, "I'll go to the bottom of the lake to eat it!" So he did, and another one said, "I'll have to go down as well; otherwise he'll eat it all by himself!" Another followed, then yet another one, so that eventually all twelve of them went down to the bottom, and that's where they still are—eating their gruel.

*Old Russian measure of weight, approximately 16.38 kilograms.

The Dog Mouser

There were so many mice in the numskulls' house that you could see them run around the farmhouse-kitchen even in the daytime. Once a wanderer who had a cat in his knapsack, happened to come by. Spotting the cat through a tear in the knapsack, the numskulls asked, "What kind of a living creature is that?"

"This is a dog mouser", said the man.

"Well, does it kill any mice, that one?"

"It kills as many as it can once it's put amongst the mice".

So they asked the animal's price. "How much would that dog mouser cost?" "One hundred roubles", the man said. The numskulls wanted to let the dog mouser down on the floor and see if it killed any mice. Well, once down on the floor, it killed all it could. They bought the dog then from the old man but told him that they didn't have so much money, not the one hundred roubles, but they did have fifty. The man said, "Well, you can owe me the rest, as long as I get the fifty now".

The man took his leave and left the dog mouser with the numskulls. But they'd forgotten to ask the man what to feed the dog mouser. So they told a boy to run after the man and call, "What should the dog mouser be fed with, when the mice are finished?" Well, the man, pleased with the amount of money he got, called back, "Whatever it wants, whatever it wants!"

When the boy returned to the farmhouse-kitchen,

the old man asked him, "What did he say to feed it with?" The boy said, "Well, he said that it kills men when the mice are finished". The boy had misheard the wanderer. That very moment they caught the dog mouser and took it to the sauna. They set the sauna alight from the outside, as they were going to kill the animal this way. They forgot that the window had been left ajar, and when the sauna was in flames, the dog mouser jumped out into the farmyard through the open window and ran off into the woods. And so the numskulls burnt their house and the whole manor in this way.

Then the numskulls bought another house nearby, as they had burnt their own house. The dog mouser had returned by itself and was now on the roof of the stables. They soon noticed it up on the roof, and they tried to stop it getting away with long poles while others were setting the stables alight. When the building was well aflame, the cat ran for its life, running at a hell of a pace towards a man who thought it was going to eat him. This is how the numskulls burnt their second home and since then got scattered around the world, and they've been homeless ever since.

Boys Swimming in the Rye-Field

nce there were six boys. They thought it would be a good idea to go for a swim. "Let's do that, by all means", replied the others. The wind was blowing very hard, and the rye, not quite ripe yet, was rippling in the wind. The boys got undressed and jumped into the rye for a swim.

After swimming they got dressed again. "How many were we when we left?" asked one of them. "There were six of us", replied Pekko.

"Well, let's check how many we are—if we're all here".

One of them began to count and only found five. Each then, one by one, took a turn at counting, and all came to the same result: five. The last count was followed by much sobbing and crying. "What a miserable swimming-trip we've had, now that one of us has drowned! There were six of us when we left, but now there's only five!"

A gentleman rode by and, seeing the boys sobbing miserably, brought his horse to a halt. "What is the matter with you, boys?" asked the gentleman. "Well", replied one, "there were six of us when we went to swim, but now there are only five!"

"I see, so there were six of you", said the gentleman.

"That's right, there were definitely six of us before", said one of the boys, "but now there's only five of us". The gentleman said, "Count aloud this time; see how many you are!" They began counting and only got to five, as no-one had included himself in the counting.

"Yes, indeed, that is a sad thing", said the gentleman, "that one of you has drowned. It's not surprising that you are crying. Perhaps you should go and search for the body, it might well bite on a large hook". The gentleman had realised that the boys were slow-witted, and said, "What simpletons you all are, in every way!" There was some cow dung on the road. "Now, there's no other way round it; since you will not understand any other way, each of you must press your nose into the dung—one by one!"

The boys did as they were told. "Well, look for yourselves now, how many nose impressions are there", said the travelling gentleman. Well, they counted them and found all six. No-one had drowned at all.

The Search for Three Fools

nce there lived a man and a woman who had a boy and a girl. They lived by a lake. One day the daughter went to wash some clothes, and as she was washing she thought, "If there was an island, and on that island there was a house, and in that house there was a boy, and the boy would marry me, and we would have a son, and he would start yearning to visit his grandparents and then he'd cross the lake and drown". Then she began to cry.

Her mother came to her and said, "Why do you cry?"

"The reason why I was crying is this: if there was an island and on that island there was a boy and that boy would marry me, then I'd have a son and he'd get a desire to visit his grandparents, and then he'd cross the lake and drown".

And they both began to cry. The son came over, and said, "Why are you crying?"

"This is what we're crying about: if there was an island, and on that island there was a house and in that house there was be a boy and he would marry me and I would have a son, and he'd get a desire to visit his grandparents and then he'd cross the lake and drown".

The boy said, "I'll have to go now, and I'll not return until I have found three fools such as you!"

And off he went, he walked for a while and heard some mumbling by the roadside. He walked towards the noise. He saw a man and a woman who had cooked some porridge and kept going into the storehouse for a knob of butter for every single mouthful. The boy said, "Why on earth are you toiling like this?"

"Well, we're toiling because we're eating porridge and we have to go to the storehouse for the butter".

"I'll show you how to put a knob of butter into the eye of the porridge".

The boy fetched some butter from the storehouse and put it in the eye of the porridge, and for this he was given a hundred marks. Off he went again, and after a while hears some mumbling again from the roadside. He went over and saw how an old man was carrying daylight in a sack into his farmhouse. The boy stopped and asked, "Why are you toiling like this?"

"Well, I'm carrying daylight into my house".

"What will you give me, if I get light into your house?"

"I'll give you two hundred marks!"

The boy set about making a window, and received his two hundred marks. He went off again, and soon heard some more mumbling by the roadside. He walked towards the noise and saw how an old soldier was trying to jump into his trousers.

"Why are you toiling like this?" asked the boy.

"Well, I'm putting my trousers on".

"That's not the way to get your trousers on!"

"Well, how do you do it then?"

"What will you give me, if I teach you how to get your trousers on?"

"Well, three hundred marks!"

The boy led the soldier to a bench, took his trousers and put them on the soldier. And for this the boy was given three hundred marks and then he remembered that it was time to go home, and he went.

⌣ ⌣ ⌣

The Man who did the Housework

There was a man called Heikki who had a farm. During the harvest he complained to his wife how little work she did at home. One morning, the wife went to the field and left Heikki home to do the chores.

First, he carried the milk churns into the farmhouse kitchen and began churning butter from the milk. When the milk had turned to butter, it occurred to him that he needed to fetch some water from the well. While fetching the water, the pig had knocked the churn over in the kitchen. Now he had to go and get new churns and began churning butter again.

Then it was time to cook the porridge for the farm labourers for their breakfast. He poured the water he had just drawn into a pot for the porridge, and then went back to the well to fetch more water to rinse the butter. Their small child was crying in the cradle, but the father dared not leave it in the kitchen in case it might fall out, and so he secured the cradle. He then remembered how the pig had knocked the milk churn over and decided not to leave the churn in the kitchen. Instead, he tied the churn to his back and then went to fetch some water from the well. As he was bending over the well, the milk and butter fell from the churn into the well. He then returned indoors to cook the porridge, and the child in the cradle began crying, as it was thirsty. And so the man went to the cellar for some beer, but as he was pouring the beer, he heard the child fall from the cradle. In all his rush he forgot to fasten the stopper on the beer-barrel, so while he was tending the child, all the beer ran out of the barrel.

Then he remembered that the cow was in the cowshed without any straw. He decided to take the cow up onto the farmhouse roof to feed, as the roof was covered in turf. But then it dawned on him that the cow might fall off the roof, and so to prevent this happening, he tied one end of a rope to the cow's leg and pushed the other end through the chimney pot into the kitchen and secured it to his own leg, and went back to cooking the porridge. While he was busy with the housework, the farm labourers in the field had grown impatient waiting for their breakfast, which was now very late, and so decided to leave for the farmhouse. When they arrived at the house, they saw that the cow had fallen from the roof which had in turn pulled Heikki up the chimney. The harvesters rushed into the farmyard and, wishing to save the cow's life, yet unaware of Heikki's predicament, cut the rope. The suspended Heikki fell straight into the pot full of boiling porridge. And that is how Heikki's worries about his wife's lack of housework came to an end.

Two Women, a Mouse and the Gold Coins

nce two women were walking down the street. One of them had good eyesight, the other one had poor eyes. They happened to be passing the king's window, which was open, and the king was looking out. When the goodsighted woman noticed the king, she said, "The good king will help". When the bad-sighted woman heard this, she said, "The king does no such thing, it's God who helps".

The king invited them into his court and put them in a room by themselves. He then put a mouse under a dish so that the women couldn't see it. Then on his way out of the room he said to the women, "You mustn't look under the dish".

But when the king left the room, the good-sighted woman looked under the dish, and the mouse escaped. On his return the king looked under the dish and saw that the mouse was no longer there. The good-sighted woman confessed to having had a look.

Then the king ordered two cakes to be baked—a big one and a small one—and he told the baker to fill the smaller cake with plenty of gold coins. When the women were leaving the court, the king gave the bigger cake to the poor-sighted woman and the smaller one to the good-sighted woman. After they had walked some distance from the court, the goodsighted woman said, "Let's change cakes". To which the poor-sighted woman replied, "I don't mind if we do". So they changed the cakes over.

While she ate the cake, the poor-sighted woman kept picking gold coins out of the cake and putting them into her pocket. The good-sighted woman wondered at what the other one was picking. "There are gold coins inside this cake", she said. To which the good-sighted woman replied, "We'll break off our deal". "No, we won't!" said the bad-sighted one.

So they began to argue and, as they were unable to finish it, the women decided to go over to the king and ask for his counsel. The king said, "A deal is a deal. You can't go back on it now. Remember it's not the king who helps, but the good God".

The Boy who Grew Up in a Barrel

There was once a father who had reared his son in a barrel, so that he would never know anything about the wicked ways of the world. When the father believed his son to be sufficiently strong, he took him out of the barrel. But when the boy had come out of the barrel and saw some girls walking past the window, he asked his father, "What are they?" "They're geese", said the father, feeling rather sad and thinking to himself, "Dear me, how nature gets the better of teaching!"

One day the father sent his son to sell butter and advised him, "If you meet a red man with a white wreath round his neck that will be the merchant, and you should offer the butter to him; but should you meet a black man wearing a white collar that will be the parson and you should offer him the butter". The boy went off and when he saw a verst-post* by the side of the road, he thought it was the merchant and offered him some butter; but to no avail. The boy then spotted a hole on the side of the post, put the butter there and went home.

When his father asked him, "Where's the money, then?", the son replied, "He never mentioned anything about money". Now the father told his son to go back and collect the money. The boy went and asked the verst-post for the money, but as it gave him none, the boy took a piece of wood from the forest and began beating the post with it. The post fell to the ground, whereupon the boy found a treasure trove with a large amount of money. When the boy took the money to his father, he was greatly pleased and promised to let his son go and sell butter once more.

The next time the boy met a dog. Thinking that this was the parson, the boy gave the butter to the dog and went home. As he had returned home without the money, the boy again had to return for it, but it was no use. The dog had disappeared, and now the father got really angry and told his son that he wouldn't be allowed to go and sell butter any more.

The boy had heard the young folk talk about sex, and so he went to his father to ask for it. Now the father became very sad, but realising that nothing

*A wooden post marker showing distance in versts.

154

could be done about the situation, he eventually said to his son, "Take this load of firewood into town and ask for sex in return!" The boy took the firewood into town and when asked, "What's the cost?" the boy replied to everybody, "Sex!" But as nobody was interested in buying the firewood from him, the boy decided to return home. On his way, however, he stopped off at one more house to offer his firewood. As the boy entered through the gateway, a large whore promptly asked him, "What do you want for your logs?" "Sex", answered the boy sprightly. "Oh, you'll get that all right; undo your load and step inside", she added. The boy did as he was told and went into the house. Meanwhile, the whore had prepared the bed and offered him some spirits. The boy gulped the drink down in one go and asked the whore, "Is this what it's like then?" "Yes", she answered hurriedly. Hearing this the boy left for home.

After a while the boy went to his father again and this time, he asked to be married. And as the father saw that to refuse his son's request would be to no avail, he decided to find a bride for the boy. At the wedding the parson allowed a bottle of spirits to be passed around, as was the custom. The boy called out, "Let me have some sex, too!" The parson, hearing this, asked that the young couple be taken into another room. The boy wouldn't budge and kept shouting aloud, "I had it in my mouth in town". They were quickly taken into the other room, where the parson explained the secrets of married life to them.

Today the couple are living happily, and the father has realised that "Nature is the better teacher". And so he never ever reared another son in a barrel again.

The Famished Parson

parson had lived a long time without marrying. His assistant said to him, "Isn't it high time you got married?" "Oh, I'd like to get married, indeed I would, but I can't find a woman who only eats one bean a day", replied the parson. "One of my daughters eats a great deal, but the other one eats nothing but one bean a day", said the assistant.

The parson married his assistant's daughter. Her father kept feeding her for a long time but eventually turned to his daughter, "I can't be bothered to feed you any longer". So the parson's wife went hungry for a few days, while her father tried to think of a way to save his daughter from hunger.

At long last the assistant went to the parson and asked him to go hunting for wild birds. The parson said, "Let's take some food with us". But his assistant said, "There's no need for that", but at the same time put some bread and cheese in his pocket without the parson's knowledge. They then went hunting. When the evening was already approaching, they came across a dead horse which had already rotted to pieces. Secretly, the assistant put a piece of cheese into his mouth. The parson asked, "What are you eating? I feel really hungry myself". "I took a bone from the carcass and picked it", said the assistant.

Then the parson took a bone and started picking it but soon threw it away, saying, "I'm not eating anything that smells so much". By then it was getting dark, so they stopped at a house for the night. When the supper was being prepared the assistant said to the parson, "In this house it's customary to be called to the table three times", whereas he told the hostess that the parson only needs to be called once. "If he doesn't come on the first call, the food should be cleared off the table", he added.

When the food was ready, the hostess invited the parson and his assistant to the table. The assistant went immediately, but the parson stayed behind waiting for the second and the third calls. As the assistant was eating, the parson winked at the man meaning for him to bring some food over. But the assistant carried on eating and didn't bring a single morsel over. When he had finished, the parson said, "You didn't bring me any food even though I kept winking at you". The assistant replied, "I thought you meant that I should keep eating—to fill myself up well".

Then it was time to go to bed. But the parson, who was extremely hungry, watched carefully where the food was put away so that he could go and eat later. When the others were asleep, the parson, who now knew that there was a big dish of beans on the stove, said to his assistant, "If I went to eat from the cauldron over there on the stove, how can I find my way back to my bed, as the house is so dark?"

"Oh, I know how to get round this one", replied the assistant, and fetched some string from the doorway, tied one end to the foot of the bed and put the other end in the parson's hand and said, "Hold this string and you'll find your way back". Holding the string in his hand the parson went over to the pot. But while the parson was eating, his assistant tied the other end of string to the foot of the bed where the farmer and his wife were sleeping. When the parson had satisfied his hunger, he took one more ladleful for his assistant and followed the string which led him to the bed of his hosts. When he got to their bed, the farmer's wife extended her arm in her sleep and tipped the ladleful of beans over with her hand, and it all fell into the bed. The assistant heard this and fetched the parson to his own bed.

After a while the farmer woke up and began scolding his wife, saying, "You have made a mess in the bed; you'd better go and clean yourself up, or even our guests will laugh at you when they see you in the morning". The wife went into the farmyard to wash herself. In the meanwhile the parson had become thirsty and said to his assitant, "Where can I get a drink?" The assistant said, "Over there on the bench there are two jugs; one has beer in it, the other one has buttermilk. Try with your finger which one's the beer before you drink it".

The parson went over to the bench and shoved his hand into the mouth of one of the jugs, which turned out to be so tight that he couldn't get his hand out again. The parson went over to his assistant to ask him how he could free his hand from the jug. "Go into the farmyard; there is a grey rock in front of the steps; break the jug against it".

The parson did this, but what he thought to be the rock was the farmer's wife, who was out there washing herself. When the parson had broken the jug against the farmer's wife, she cried out, "Please, dear guest, don't hit me any more; I'll never soil my bed again!" Then the parson went back to bed, and he and his assistant slept till the morning.

And that's all.

Notes

The stories translated in this volume are numbered 1–50, with cross-references to page, the Finnish title (if any), Tale Type number, available information on the circumstances and individuals involved in the transmission and recording of the tale, and the source of the translated text.

AT   Aarne-Thompson number. The Tale Type number assigned to the story in Stith Thompson, *The Types of the Folk-Tale: Antti Aarne's Verzeichnis der Märchentypen Translated and Enlarged*, Folklore Fellows Communications 74 (Helsinki, 1961).

(N)   Narrator with available biographical details and background on the transmission of the tale.

(P)   Place and date of collection.

(C)   Collector and/or editor.

[1]   From Pirkko-Liisa Rausmaa, ed., *Suomalaiset kansansadut 1. Ihmesadut*, 2nd rev. ed. (Helsinki: Suomalaisen Kirjallisuuden Seura, 1988).

[2]   From Pirkko-Liisa Rausmaa, ed., *Suomalaiset kansansadut 2. Legendat ja novellisadut* (Helsinki: Suomalaisen Kirjallisuuden Seura, 1982).

[3]   From Pirkko-Liisa Rausmaa, ed., *Suomalaiset kansansadut 3. Sadut tyhmästä paholaisesta* (Helsinki: Suomalaisen Kirjallisuuden Seura, 1990).

[4]   From Eero Salmelainen, ed., *Suomen Kansan Satuja ja Tarinoita* [1852–1866], 8th ed. (Helsinki: Suomalaisen Kirjallisuuden Seura, 1989).

[5]   From the Manuscript Collection of the Folklore Archive, Suomalaisen Kirjallisuuden Seura, Helsinki, Finland.

1. The Rabbit, the Wolf, the Fox and the Bear Caught in a Pit (p. 1). *Jänis, susi, repo ja karhu yhtenä maahaudassa*. AT 20A. (P) Toksova, Ingria, 1847. (C) Eero Salmelainen/D.E.D. Europaeus. [4].

2. The Fox as Nursemaid (p. 2). Untitled in ms. AT 37. (N) Olga Elliida Hiekkanen, age 16, from Jämsa. (P) Jämsä, 1888. (C) Lilli Lilius. [5].

3. The Fox, the Wolf and the Lion (p. 4). *Kettu, susi ja jalopeura*. AT 50. (P) Häme, 1854. (C) Eero Salmelainen/O. Palander. [4].

4. The Dog's Document (p. 5). *Koiran pöytäkirja*. AT 102 + AT 104 + AT 200. (N) Santra Kemppainen, age 18, from Korpinvaara. (P) Ristijärvi, 1882. (C) Kaarle Krohn. [5].

An Anthology of Finnish Folktales

5. **The Pig and the Squirrel** (p. 7). *Sika ja orava.* AT 120. (P) Rautalampi, 1883. (C) Juho Nikulainen. [5].

6. **The Wedding Roast** (p. 8). *Hääpaisti.* AT 130B. (N) Miina Toivonen, age 20, from the village of Heinijärvi in the parish of Hämeenkyrö. (P) Hämeenkyrö, 1889. (C) Vihtori Kievari. [5].

7. **The Reward of the Benefactor** (p. 11). *Hyväntekijän palkka.* AT 155. (N) F.O. Viitanen, age 14; heard from Kaarle Schylander, age 45, from Häijää. (P) Mouhijärvi, Mustianoja, 1895. (C) T.V. Laine. [5].

8. **Aal, Taal and Everaal** (p. 13). *Aal, Taal ja Everaal.* AT 300. (N) Annastiina Korkeamäki, age 56; heard as a child. (P) Tyrvää, Vammala, 1890. (C) Heikki Ojansuu. [1].

9. **The Three Missing Princesses** (p. 20). *Kolme kadonnutta kuninkaantytärtä.* AT 301A. (N) Eevertti Okkonen, the young son at the Kokkovaara Inn. (P) Sotkamo, Nuasjärvi, 1880. (C) Jooseppi Mustakallio. [1].

10. **The Three Brothers** (p. 26). *Kolme veljestä.* AT 303. (N) Karl Walden, age 24. (P) Loppi, Pilpala, 1887. (C) K.F. Andersson. [1].

11. **Three Brothers Imprisoned by the Devil** (p. 33). *Kolme veljestä pirun vankeina.* AT 327G + AT 1121 + AT 1653B. (N) Miina Toivonen, age 20. (P) Hämeenkyrö, Heinijärvi, 1889. (C) Vihtori Kievari. [1].

12. **The Smith and the Devil** (p. 37). *Seppä ja piru.* AT 330A. (P) Hankasalmi, 1889. (C) V. Manninen. [1].

13. **The Bird Bride** (p. 40). *Lintumorsian.* AT 402. (N) Este Nykyttäjä, mid-50s. (P) Kontokki, Akonlahti, 1880. (C) Jooseppi Mustakallio. [1].

14. **The Maiden Who Rose From the Sea** (p. 42). *Merestä-nousija-neito.* AT 403A. (P) (1) Viena, East Karelia, 1837 (2) Uhtua, 1836. (C) (1) Eero Salmelainen/Elias Lönnrot (2) J. Fr. Cajan. [4].

15. **The Death of the Wicked Witch** (p. 54). *Syöjättären kuolema.* AT 403A. (P) Nurmes, 1897. (C) A. Huotari. [5].

16. **The Devoted Orphans** (p. 56). Untitled in ms. AT 403A. (N) Aili Kiviranta, age 14. (P) Impilahti, Hippola, 1938. [5].

17. **The Castle of Snakes** (p. 59). *Käärmeitten linna.* AT 425C. (N) VanhaEeki, age 58. (P) Eurajoki, 1891. (C) Tuomas Tuomi. [1].

18. **Antti Puuhaara** (p. 63). *Antti Puuhaara.* AT 461. (P) Tuulos, Kuroevesi, 1850. (C) Eino Salmelainen/A.E. Nylander. [4].

19. **The Old Man's Daughter and the Old Woman's Daughters** (p. 78). *Ukon tytär ja akan tyttäret.* AT 480. (P) Kärkölä, 1887. (C) K.F. Andersson. [1].

20. **Tittulas Tuuree** (p. 82). *Tittulas Tuuree.* AT 500. (N) Jukka Häkkinen, age 36, a farm-hand at a vicarage. (P) Saarijärvi village, 1885. (C) Lilli Lilius. [1].

21. **The Pig Maid** (p. 84). Untitled in ms. AT 510A. (N) Olga Koskinen, age 14, from Juokatti, Jämsä. (P) Jämsä, 1888. (C) Lilli Lilius. [4].

22. **A Disguised Woman as the King's Brother-in-Law** (p. 86). *Nainen kuninkaan vävynä.* AT 514. (N) Johan Hartman [Österholm], age 75; heard at Valamo Monastery. (P) Merikarvia, Köörtilä, 1889. (C) Fr. V. Tommila. [1].

23. **The Witch and the Sister of Nine Brothers** (p. 92). *Syöjätär ja yhdeksän veljen sisar.* AT 533. (P) Ilomantsi, 1845. (C) D.E.D. Europaeus. [1].

24. **The Farting Stone** (p. 95). *Pierukivi.* AT 593. (N) Anni Lampola, age 17. (P) Nakkila, 1889. (C) F.O. Lampola. [1].

25. **The Three Doctors** (p. 97). *Kolme lääkäriä.* AT 660). (N) Laima Rankonen, age 15, from Lavia village; heard from Liisa Hakala in the same village. (P) Lavia, 1890. (C) Vihtori Kievari. [5].

26. **The Cat Child** (p. 99). *Kissa-lapsi.* AT 708. (P) Lohja, 1887. (C) Mathilda Österberg. [1].

27. **The King's Son on his Way to Marry** (p. 102). *Kuninkaanpojan naimatie.* AT 851. (P) Sahalahti, Ilola, 1850. (C) A.E. Nylander. [2].

28. **The Clever Girl at the Inn** (p. 104). *Viisas kestikievarin tyttö.* AT 875. (N) Iivana Onoila, alias Iivana Onessima. (P) Suistamo, Suurarka, 1915. (C) Eino Kemppainen. [2].

29. **Half a Man and a Horse's Head** (p. 108). *Puoli miestä ja hevosen pää.* AT 921. (N) Tahvo Hotti, crofter, age 70; heard in childhood from his father. (P) Haukivuori, Pohjalahti, 1884. (C) O. Hynninen. [2].

30. **The Farmer's Weather Prediction** (p. 111). *Talonpojan sääennustus.* AT 921C*. (N) Joha Prästi, age 60. (P) Marttila, Simola, 1886. (C) Aleksander Lindqvist. [2].

31. **The Sailor and the Parson** (p. 113). *Merimies ja pappi.* AT 921D. (N) Josef Vesterbakka. (P) Karvia, 1852. (C) Berndt Aug. Paldani. [2].

32. **The Merchant's Son Casts His Net** (p. 114). *Kauppiaanpoika kokee verkkonsa.* AT 926C*. (N) Otteliana Saxman, widow, age 63; heard from her late mother in Korpilahti. (P) Jyväskylä, 1893. (C) O. Ahti. [2].

33. **The Prophecy of Murder and Incest** (p. 117). *Ennustus murhasta ja sukurutsasta.* AT 931 + AT 756. (N) Herman Ketonen, age 28; heard from an East Karelian peddler from the village of Heikkilä in Archangel(?). (P) Teisko, 1903. (C) N. Ruusunen. [2].

34. **The Stonemason's Apprentice as a Bank Robber** (p. 122). *Muurarinkisälli pankkirosvona.* AT 950. (N) Albert Wikstedt, age 56, in Kärkölä. (P) Mäntsälä, 1887. (C) K.F. Andersson. [2].

35. **The Helsinki Academy** (p. 128). *Helsingin akatemia.* AT 956A. (P) Asikkala, 1885. (C) Olga Lampinen. [2].

36. **The Devil Buys Wood** (p. 130). *Piru ostaa metsää.* AT 1048. (N) Backman, a tailor from Haapakimola. (P) Iitti, 1890. (C) Taavi Puttila. [2].

37. **The Unknown Bird** (p. 130). *Tuntematon lintu.* AT 1092. (P) Mikkeli district, 1882. (C) A. Lampinen. [5].

An Anthology of Finnish Folktales

38. **The Devil Eats his Thingy** (p. 132). *Piru syö värkkinsä.* AT 1133. (N) Eerikki Pietikäinen, age 24. (P) Pyhäjärvi Ol, 1884. (C) Kaarle Krohn. [3].

39. **Four Sámi in the Giant's Gorge** (p. 134). *Neljä lappalaista jättiläisen rotkossa.* AT 1137. (N) Matti Raja, age 18, from Pitkänmaa village; heard from Vihtori Petäjys of Petäjyskylä. (P) Jalasjärvi, 1889. (C) Herman Brandt. [3].

40. **The First Gun** (p. 136). *Ensimmäinen pyssy.* AT 1228. (N) Eeri Penno/ Pento. (P) Sääksmäki, Akaa, 1884. (C) K.K. Aalto. [5].

41. **The Branch Cutter** (p. 137). *Oksan hakkaaja.* AT 1240 + AT 1313A. (N) Kristian Forsberg, age 31, from the village of Koukki in Virolahti, where he heard the tale. (P) Vehkalahti, Pampyöli, 1889. (C) Vihtori Alava. [5].

42. **The Bustle of the Numskulls** (p. 138). *Hölmöläisten touhuja.* AT 1243 + AT 1245 + AT 1290 + AT 1287 + AT 1241. (N) Vihtori Aronen, age 30, labourer. (P) Längelmäki, Kalkku, 1892. (C) E.A. Tunkelo [Ekman]. [5].

43. **The Twelve Brothers** (p. 141). *Kaksitoista veljestä.* AT 1275 + AT 1212 + AT 1260. (N) Juhana Moilanen, age 39; heard in his own village as small boy. (P) Suomussalmi, Keinälänniemi, 1882. (C) Kaarle Krohn. [5].

44. **The Dog Mouser** (p. 144). *Hiirikoira,* AT 1281. (N) Juho Pihlainen, age 50. (P) Railway works yard on the Kotka-Kouvola track, Saarijärvi, 1889. (C) Vihtori Alava. [5].

45. **Boys Swimming in the Rye-Field** (p. 146). *Pojat uivat ruispellossa.* AT 1290 + AT 1287. (N) Albert Wikstedt, age 56. (P) Mäntsälä. (C) K.F. Andersson. [5].

46. **The Search for Three Fools** (p. 148). *Kolmen hupsun etsintä.* AT 1450 + AT 1384 + AT 1263 + AT 1245 + AT 1286. (N) Iro Lesojeff. (P) Kivijärvi, Viena, Eastern Karelia, 1913. (C) Niku Marttini. [5].

47. **The Man Who Did the Housework** (p. 150). Untitled in ms. AT 1408. (N) Olli Kiiskinen, age 16, from Kumpuranta. (P) Kerimäki, 1891. (C) Lilli Lilius. [5].

48. **Two Women, A Mouse and Gold Coins** (p. 152). *Kaksi akkaa, hiiri vadin alla, kultarahoja kakossa.* AT 1416 + AT 841. (N) Kaarle Peltoniemi, age 21; heard from Matti Mellin in his own village. (P) Hämeenkyrö, Kuotila, 1890. (C) Vihtori Kievari. [5].

49. **The Boy Who Grew Up in a Barrel** (p. 153). *Tynnyrissä kasvatettu poika,* AT 1642 + AT 1686*. (N) Juho Skogström, age 20; heard from W. Kivimäki, age 41. (P) Mouhijärvi, Häijää, 1893. (C) T.V. Laine. [5].

50. **The Famished Parson** (p. 156). *Pappi nälänhädässä.* AT 1775. (N) Santra Kustaantytär, age 30, from the village of Kyröspohja in Hämeenkyrö parish. (P) Hämeenkyrö, 1889. (C) Vihtori Kievari. [5].

Index of Narrators and Collectors

Numbers refer to the ordering of the tales in the above notes. N = Narrator; C = Collector and/or editor.

Index of Tale Types

welsh academic press

The Medieval Dragon
The Nature of the Beast in Germanic Literature

Joyce Tally Lionarons

Examining how dragons are portrayed in the epic masterworks, *Beowulf* (Old English), *Vǫlsunga saga* (Icelandic), *Das Nibelungenlied* (Middle High German), and *þiðrekr saga af Bern* (Old Norwegian), Joyce Tally Lionarons explores the relationship between the dragons of medieval Germanic literature and the chaos monsters of Indo-European myth, while searching for the reasons behind the often uncanny similarity between the dragons and their antagonists, the dragon-slayers.

978-1-86057-1602	256pp	£19.99	PB
978-1-86057-1619	256pp	£19.99	EBK

The Saga of Hávarður of Ísafjörður

E. Paul Durrenburger and Dorothy Durrenburger

Written between 1300 and 1350, *The Saga of Hávarður of Ísafjörður* is a ninth-century Icelandic tale of conflict over sheep and stranded whales, magic and ghosts, seduction, murder, torture and revenge.

The first English translation of the saga since 1906, and the only one to remain faithful to the original text, Paul and Dorothy Durrenburger's masterful study not only preserves the integrity of the saga as a cultural artifact, but their definitive introduction and notes provide the scholarly context and anthropological perspective that are essential to acquiring a comprehensive understanding of the saga and medieval Icelandic society.

978-1-86057-1640	104pp	£19.99	PB
978-1-86057-1657	104pp	£19.99	EBK

welsh academic press

The Saga of Bjorn
Champion of the Men of Hitardale

Translated, with Introduction and Notes, by

Alison Finlay

"The Saga of Bjorn, Champion of the Hitardale Men, is not as well known as it should be and this new English translation deserves a warm welcome."
Professor Peter Foote,
Dept of Scandinavian Studies, University College London

"This translation, with a full accounting for the literary-historical background of the saga, will set the standard for the next round of English translations."
Professor Theodore Andersson
Dept of Germanic Studies, Indiana University

One of the earliest and most substantial of the Icelandic sagas, *The Saga of Bjorn (Bjarnar saga hitdaelakappa)* is an epic tale of a love rivalry between two poets, Bjorn and Thord, that results in Bjorn's ultimate betrayal and death.

Dating from the period between 1000 and 1025, and located in the Snæfellsnes region of Iceland, the saga describes how Thord (*Þórðr skáld Kolbeinsson*) reneges on his promise to deliver Bjorn's marriage proposal to Oddny (*Oddný Þorkelsdóttir*), then persuades her that Bjorn is dead and marries Oddny himself. A furious and distraught Bjorn seeks retribution against his former friend but is killed in a heroic battle against Thord and twenty-four of his warriors.

Finlay's acclaimed translation of 14th and 17th century manuscripts, comprehensive introduction and extensive notes of this much neglected text also surveys the saga genre and investigates its relationship with other European literature.

Alison Finlay is a retired Professor of Medieval English and Icelandic Literature at Birkbeck College, University of London.

978-1-86057-1626   160pp   £19.99   PB
978-1-86057-1633   160pp   £19.99   EBK

www.ingramcontent.com/pod-product-compliance
Lightning Source LLC
Chambersburg PA
CBHW071125280326
41935CB00010B/1119